YOUR COMPREHENSIVE TRAINING GUIDE TO

PUPPIES

SURVIVING THE FIRST SIX MONTHS

LARRY W. NEILSON

YOUR COMPREHENSIVE TRAINING GUIDE TO

PUPPIES

SURVIVING THE FIRST SIX MONTHS

LARRY W. NEILSON

Your Comprehensive Training Guide to Puppies: Surviving the First Six Months

© 2017 by Larry W. Neilson

Paperback ISBN: 978-1-7751077-0-5

Additional copies of this book may be ordered by visiting the PPG Online Bookstore at:

★PolishedPublishingGroup
shop.polishedpublishinggroup.com

Due to the dynamic nature of the Internet, any website addresses mentioned within this book might have been changed or discontinued since its publication.

By adhering to the methods described within this book, you will inevitably forge an enduring partnership with your puppy that will last a lifetime. You will uncover the time tested and proven tools of the trade developed, refined, and implemented by the author, Larry Neilson, owner and head trainer of Konfident Kanines Inc., (www.konfidentkanines.com)—the same "treat free" tools and techniques he has used to train and rehabilitate countless dogs over the course of the last four decades.

Table of Contents

Acknowledgements

The generous contributions to this book made through conversations with Dr. Ingrid Rozema of the Eastern Slopes Veterinary Clinic (www.easternslopesvet.com) in Black Diamond, Alberta; the late Brent Brooks of Brooks Labrador Retrievers in Lucas, Texas; and Jan Zerebeski of Janzhaus German Shepherds (www.janzhaus.com) in Sylvan Lake, Alberta, are invaluable.

To all my valued clients who have supported my decision to write this book, and a special thank you to Rhonda Hey and my partner Karen for their unselfish giving of their time in assisting in the proofreading of this book.

The nutritional chapter within this book would not have been possible without the support of well-known author, trainer, and canine nutritional expert Wendy Volhard (www.volhard.com) of the United States. Wendy's kindness and permission to use her nutritional material in this book underlines her confidence in her abilities and willingness to continue to contribute to canine betterment throughout the globe.

The photos contained throughout the book simply would not have been possible without the commitment to quality and perseverance of my life partner Karen St-Germain of Frames of Life Photography.

This book has been enhanced by their respected and valued professional contributions.

Over the years, I have been exposed to countless puppies and an even greater number of well-meaning people who, although they started out with good intentions for their puppy, quickly found themselves in over their heads. Many of my former customers have unknowingly contributed to this book, as have my own personal experiences. I respectfully acknowledge that there is an almost infinite supply of puppy training guides on the market today. It is not my intention to discredit one or any of those views in any way, nor do I claim that I am always right and others are wrong. I simply believe there are many approaches to puppy training, and I maintain some are much more effective than others. It is my belief that the contents of this book will not only serve to guide you through any and all of the challenges that may arise during the first six months of your puppy's life, but will also assist you in a way that is not only humane but fun, and, most importantly, meaningful to your puppy, as well.

About the Author

Larry Neilson moved to the Calgary, Alberta, area of Canada from Northwestern Ontario almost four decades ago. A heavy duty maintenance technician by trade, Larry's love of animals has been a life-long passion. His genuine love for and interest in dogs resulted in his being around or owning these fascinating animals for most of his life. When he was quite young, it was pointed out to him that it was obvious he had an uncanny ability to communicate with dogs in a way that most others could not and in a manner that dogs clearly understood and respected.

Larry Neilson is a certified dog trainer, certified advanced dog trainer, certified dog trainer Instructor, and trainer evaluator with many decades of hands on experience working with thousands of dogs and handlers of all ages and breeds. Larry is an advocate of "balanced training" and firmly believes that to become a good canine teacher, we must first genuinely respect the dog enough to provide the dog ample opportunity to use its mind and make decisions on its own. It is with a sense of considerable but humble pride, that Larry is quite proud of the fact that his expertise is sought out by many people who will travel great distances to seek his assistance with their beloved canines that are exhibiting behaviours others were unable to help them with.

For several years, Larry owned and operated a successful pet supply store complete with a busy grooming and training facility.

Larry has been involved in the martial arts for many years, a mental discipline that he relies heavily on when working with dogs. The mind control and patience developed while studying the philosophy of Kung Fu is of significant benefit when working with dogs and their handlers alike. When around Larry, the topic of dogs is sure to come up as he lives and breathes dogs. Larry currently resides in Calgary, Alberta, with his partner Karen and their golden retriever Ryder.

Preface

The objectives when writing Your Comprehensive Training Guide to Puppies: Surviving the First Six Months were simple: to provide effective and applicable information on positively influencing the development of a puppy over the course of its first six months of life. What you do during these first few months is critical in establishing the foundation for progressive education as your puppy develops into an adult dog. It is during this formidable puppy developmental period that you will set the stage for what will follow once your puppy leaves the puppyhood stage and enters into the adolescent and then adult stages of life. Mistakes made now will almost always manifest themselves in undesirable or possibly even dangerous behaviours later in your dog's life. There are no shortcuts to raising a well-behaved dog. Like rearing a child to become a well-mannered and responsible adult, it is not always easy; shaping a puppy's manners is no less of a challenge. For better or for worse, what you do at this stage will surely reveal itself in the adult dog.

It is of absolute importance that you understand the author's intentions behind each of the exercises described within the book. It is the author's position that dogs, be it a puppy or an adult, learn by association. Yes, of course, puppies develop their skills by repeating them as they grow and develop mentally and physically. They initially learn what to do and what not to do by attaching (associating) a consequence to any given behaviour. Once you accept this method of learning to be true, you will be on the path to understanding how nature works to ensure that the wisest and strongest survive while those who are weaker and prone to making mistakes do not. Over the past four decades, the author has focused as much, or more, on studying canine behaviours and what he refers to as "behaviour drivers" as he has to teaching dogs. This approach to working with dogs has allowed him to gain an uncanny ability to read a dog's mind and actually predict what a dog might or might not do, depending on the situations the dog is exposed to. Without attempting to delve too deeply into the infinite skills required to teach a dog, even a puppy, the author is absolutely convinced that the mechanics of training a dog, although important, pale in comparison to the importance of the energy radiated by the dog's handler or owner while teaching or being in close proximity to the dog.

During your training or teaching sessions (as the author prefers to refer to a dog's education) with your puppy, you must be completely free of anger or frustration of any kind. You must understand that if you allow these emotions to creep into your methodology, even slightly, while you are working with your puppy, then you have abandoned the teaching mode and entered into a suppressive mode. Balanced training is exactly that, balanced. If you allow yourself to radiate even the slightest amount of negative energy (anger or frustration), then you are no longer mentally balanced and the puppy will immediately pick up on your emotions. In the canine world, dogs are constantly seeking balance. In the mind of a dog, an unbalanced leader is unstable and cannot be trusted to provide structured leadership in a way that will best serve the survival of the pack as a whole. Training a dog—regardless of whether it is a puppy of six months old or less, or an older dog—requires that we remain calm and balanced at all times. Although we refer to a dog's education as training, the author prefers to refer to it as educating while forming an alliance with your puppy. Don't be fooled by those who insist that you have to demonstrate that you are the "Alpha"! How foolish is that? Yes, you must establish that you are a great leader, one who will provide structure and leadership; however, this never means that you have to be loud or abrasive, and certainly does not at any time include the slightest amount of frustration, doubt, or anger.

There is little in life more rewarding than building resilient and long lasting relationships. This includes our canine partners!

Family Planning

The importance of total family involvement when discussing the possibility of bringing a new puppy into your home cannot be over emphasized. It is not sufficient for one or two members of your family to make the decision to obtain a puppy if there are other persons within your immediate family unit. When considering the adoption of a puppy, whether it is from a breeder, pet store, neighbour, friend, or acquaintance, the consequences are long lasting, usually ten years or more. It is imperative that you consider your work schedules, travel habits, how much time your dog will be left alone, whether you are expecting a new baby, or whether perhaps one or more of the family members will be going away in the near future, maybe to college or to work elsewhere. Does any member of your family have allergic reactions to pets? It is also tremendously important to conduct open, honest, and transparent discussions regarding the breed of puppy, the size, temperament, life span, cost, availability, breed health issues if any, housing, local or housing complex bylaws, and individual responsibilities. Every family member must be part of these discussions in proportion to their age and responsibilities. It goes without saying that the parents or head of household will in all likelihood have the final say in the end decision;

however, by involving everyone, the selection and adoption process will be a unified family decision and joint responsibility from the outset.

Larry continues to successfully coach people and their puppies and dogs of all ages from all walks of life, shaping them into successful canine handlers with model canine citizens that are a joy to be around.

Learning together. Story time for puppy.

The Right Match

For the purpose of this chapter, let's assume that as a family unit you have now concluded your research, and the time is right to take the next step towards adopting a new puppy into your home. Before you arrange to go and view a single puppy, it is extremely important to do some thorough homework first. You wouldn't go out and buy a new car without doing some advance research, would you now? Keep in mind that typically a female puppy (dog) will be better with children than most male dogs. Don't be blinded by the fact that all puppies by their very nature are cute. Don't fall into the age-old trap of impulse buying based on the looks or actions of a seven- or eight-week-old puppy.

One of the first considerations I encourage those in the process of adopting a new puppy take into account is your home environment. Is your home large or small? Is it a high-rise apartment, condo, house in the suburbs, or a sprawling ranch out in the country? In any case, it is highly likely that the home you currently live in will be your home for the foreseeable future. If you live in a compact and efficient apartment at the top of a towering high-rise, a Great Dane or Irish wolfhound is probably not for you. On the opposite end of the scale, if you live out in the rugged countryside, a Pekinese with flowing hair may not be a good choice either. Whatever breed of puppy you decide upon, it should be a dog that is an appropriate physical match for your immediate environment and living accommodations. Once you as a collective family unit have reached a consensus as to the size of dog that is most appropriate for your current living arrangement and lifestyle, you might then want to consider which of the following groups of dogs may be the most appropriate for your family.

Selecting a puppy that will be a good match for your family must begin with a pretty good idea of what role your dog is going to play in your life and then doing your best to choose a dog that is suitable for your purposes. The subsequent list may assist you in picking out a dog that is right for you. Regardless of the dog you decide upon, take the time to carefully choose a puppy that is likely to meet your expectations when the dog reaches adulthood.

There are many reasons for deciding to add a dog to your family. I have listed just a few of these reasons below:

- camaraderie
- playmate for the kids
- status symbol (something I never recommend)
- a special activity, such as hunting, herding, breeding, showing in conformation, or competing in competitive events
- personal protection (not for the faint-hearted)
- a combination of the above reasons

Some dogs are able to fulfill all of these expectancies; others have more restricted abilities.

Additional factors when making your decision might include whether you prefer:

- a long- or short-hair dog (Grooming can become quite expensive and time consuming.)
- a shedding or nonshedding dog (All dogs shed: some considerably more than others.)

- a male or female dog

- a sporting or nonsporting dog (Most dogs in this group are hounds and hunting dogs.)

- a working dog such as guard dogs, sled dogs, etc. (These dogs are often heavy shedders and need ample physical and mental exercise.)

- a toy breed (Dogs in this group are good for smaller living areas but not always good with small children.)

- a terrier breed (Dogs in this group may also be listed under the toy group. Terriers, as a rule, will have a much stronger temperament and need a firm hand.)

- a hound (Dogs in this group encompass a wide range of sizes, all the way from the miniature Dachshund up to and including the massive Irish wolfhound. They are active dogs.)

- a herding dog (Dogs in this group are very intelligent and easily trained in the right hands but are usually very active dogs.)

- a purebred or mixed breed (As a rule it is easier to predict a purebred's temperament.)

The importance of devoting the time and effort necessary towards your puppy selection process cannot be overstated. The careful consideration you dedicate to matching a puppy to your personality and lifestyle will undoubtedly prove to be one of the best investments of your time and attention you could make. Any shortcuts taken here will surely come back to haunt you many times over during the years to come. Remember that all puppies are cute; do not allow your emotions to overrule your common sense.

Selecting a Veterinarian

An important factor to be considered during the decision-making process of getting a puppy is veterinary care and what traits and services you may require when seeking a veterinarian best suited to your specific requirements and personality. The time to begin your veterinary selection is before you pick your puppy up. Providing you do your homework and select a veterinarian best suited to your personality and expectations, your veterinarian can provide you with information only those in the veterinary profession can.

A good start to selecting the right veterinarian for you might begin with a call to a veterinary clinic near you. If you are lucky enough to find a veterinarian suited to you and your needs that is located close to you, then you have already made a good first step. Although the proximity to your location is important when choosing a vet, it should not be the only deciding factor. Choosing a veterinarian near you who has limited hours of service or does not treat you like a valued client will surely lead to problems down the road; thus, the reasons for calling one or more veterinary clinics before you actually pick your puppy up. If, when you call a veterinary clinic they do not make you feel comfortable on the phone, then chances are this veterinary clinic is not for you. Rely on your gut instincts. Most often they are right. Allow yourself the time you need to find a suitable veterinarian so that you don't feel rushed. Your relationship with your veterinarian is one that will span several years, so do your homework and choose a veterinarian that is not only reputable, but one that is willing to explain your puppy's needs in the short term as well as over the dog's lifetime, and in a language that you can comprehend. If veterinarians are not willing to take the time to talk with you and answer your questions before you have your puppy, chances are they will not have time to provide the service you expect and deserve once you have adopted your puppy.

Following are some things you should consider when choosing a veterinarian for your puppy:

a) Proximity. Is the veterinarian located nearby or in another county?

b) Relationship. Does the veterinarian make you feel comfortable when you call?

c) Customer service. Can you visit the clinic and observe how clients are treated when they come into the clinic? Is this how you want to be treated?

d) The cost of services. Are the costs at the clinic affordable? Veterinary services can be expensive; however, there can be a substantial variance in cost for similar services from one veterinary clinic to another.

e) Hours of operation. Do they have 24-hour service, or do they sublet these services? If not, who handles their after-hour emergencies?

f) Breed experience. Does the veterinarian you are considering have experience with your breed of dog? Often perfectly great veterinarians may not have experience with certain dog breeds.

g) Transparency. Will they give you a tour of their clinic? If not, this should raise a red flag. You should be able to arrange a tour of the facility you would be bringing your puppy to for all of its health care needs. Get a feel for the place; does it seem to be organized, clean, friendly, efficient, etc.?

h) Openness. Will they give you access to your dog's veterinary records? These records are yours, and you have every right to see them. You cannot remove the records from the veterinary clinic; however, you do have the right to review your pets' medical files on the site.

It is your pet and your vet. Select a veterinarian that makes you feel comfortable and is able to put both you and your puppy at ease.

Veterinary Care

Your puppy's first visit to the veterinarian you have chosen should include discussions about housing, nutrition, training, and any other mental and physical health concerns you may have about your puppy. It might also be a good idea to discuss the spaying or neutering of your puppy at this time so that you can plan ahead and schedule this procedure, should you decide to do so, for the time that is recommended by your veterinarian and your breeder. Puppy vaccines are very important, and all dogs should be vaccinated. The maternal antibodies transferred from the mother dog to her offspring can interfere with vaccines; therefore, it is always a good idea to discuss your puppy's vaccination needs with your veterinarian—although the issue of how often a puppy or dog needs to be vaccinated and what vaccinations are required is as controversial as it is varied. For the purpose of this book, I will provide you Dr. Ingrid Rozema's recommendations. As in every other field, the field of veterinary medicine is constantly evolving as well. Dr. Rozema explained that twenty or more years ago, vaccines were recommended every year due primarily to the fact that vaccine manufacturing companies would only test their vaccine for a one-year period. As the field of veterinary medicine continues to evolve, vaccination recommendations are changing as well. Always get your information from a reliable source, namely your vet. In the event you wish to get a second professional opinion on vaccine requirements or intervals, that option is always available to you. If a puppy is taken in for its first shots at two months of age, then it should be vaccinated again at three months and four months of age and again once it is a year old. From that point on, your dog should only require vaccinations at three- or four-year intervals or after checking titer levels to determine vaccination needs. The antibody titer test is a simple blood test that detects the presence of and measures the amount of antibodies within your puppy's blood. The quantity and diversity of antibodies correlate to the strength of the body's immune response. If the puppy gets its first shots at six months or older, the initial vaccines can be given in one shot.

Where to Buy Your Puppy

Perhaps the most controversial of all topics when one is considering adopting a puppy is the subject of where to purchase a puppy. By now I am sure that you have decided on the breed of dog most suitable for you and your family's lifestyle, so now you must decide on the source for your new puppy. This can often be a daunting task in itself. If you have decided on a purebred dog, then, of course, I would suggest you search your local, provincial, or state kennel club. This is a good place to start. I have had the privilege of meeting a well-known breeder of Labrador Retrievers near Dallas, Texas, and have visited their widely respected, family owned and operated breeding facility. I have also met with and toured Janzhaus Shepherds near Sylvan Lake, Alberta. With the knowledge and help of the late Mr. Brent Brooks and Jan Zerebeski, I have included some pertinent information that you absolutely need to have in your possession before you begin your quest to acquire a suitable puppy that will most likely meet or exceed your requirements and expectations.

Q) *What are some of the advantages of purchasing a puppy from a reputable breeder?*

A) Predictability. One of the greatest advantages of sourcing your puppy through a reputable breeder is that you have some assurances of the historical characteristics, both physical and mental, common to that breed of dog.

You will also increase the potential of obtaining a puppy that is genetically sound. You will have access to historic health clearances for that particular breeder's bloodlines.

Another advantage of selecting a kennel club registered purebred puppy is that in the event that one day should you decide to enter your puppy into obedience or conformation trials (providing the puppy is unaltered), you will be able to do so.

Q) *What are some of the disadvantages of sourcing a puppy through a breeder?*

A) There are not many, but if cost is a factor, often a puppy from a breeder may initially cost a bit more to purchase. That being said, I do not recommend that you let the cost be the only deciding factor. Often when you are dealing with a reputable breeder, the initial cost may be offset many times over during the life of the dog by avoiding health problems and associated veterinary costs over the duration of your dog's life.

Whatever you decide, don't be shy about asking questions of whomever you are considering adopting a puppy from. Do your homework thoroughly! Don't be duped into believing that just because a puppy or the breeder is registered with a kennel club that this in itself provides assurances you are dealing with a reputable breeder. A breeder's association with a kennel club means only that—that they are associated with a kennel club. That association in itself may have little or no bearing on the quality of individual breeders or the dogs they breed or raise.

Some questions you will want to ask your breeder should include:

1) What is the total cost of the puppy?

2) If the dog does not prove to be a good match for you, will they take the dog back? If so, will they refund all or a portion of the purchase cost? What are the refund conditions?

3)   Is there a written health guarantee? If so, what is guaranteed and when does the guarantee expire?

4)   Is there a deposit required? Is it refundable?

5)   If the puppy comes from afar, who pays for the shipping costs?

6)   Does the breeder own both the sire and the dam? If not, what are the breeding arrangements? Is the sire and/or dam owned, leased or otherwise?

7)   Are the sire and the dam on the property? If so, can you see them and get to meet with them?

8)   How long has the breeder been in business with that particular breed?

9)   What health issues (physical or mental) have been experienced in this bloodline?

10) Does the breeder provide follow-up advice on the proper raising of the puppy, and if so is there a cost?

11) What health issues are common to the breed?

12) Are your dogs typically good with children?

13) What food do you feed and why?

14) Do the sire and the dam have health clearances from the Orthopedic Foundation for Animals (OFA) or similar organization? If so, what clearances do they have? Eye, heart, hips, EIC (exercise induced collapse), etc.?

Some questions you might expect your breeder to ask of you may include:

1)   Are you a first-time dog owner?

2)   Have you owned this particular breed before?

3)   Why have you decided on this particular breed?

4)   What is the sex of the dog you are seeking and why?

5)   What are your goals for this dog within your family?

6) What are your goals? Are you looking for a family pet, gun dog, service dog, tracking dog, home protection dog, etc.?

7) What is your lifestyle? Are you active, inactive, outdoor orientated, or more of an indoor person?

8) Are you best suited for a high-energy dog, a low-energy dog, or a medium-energy dog? The breeder will help you decide on this based on your lifestyle.

9) What is your commitment to training your dog? A lot of good breeders are reluctant to sell to those who have no intention of training or educating their puppy so that it becomes a good canine citizen. Most reputable breeders will be able to help you select an experienced trainer that has a long and proven track record of successful training.

Be wary of any breeder who is overly eager to sell you a puppy. One good sign of a reputable and conscientious breeder is one who interviews you just as thoroughly as you will want to interview them. If the breeder you select is unwilling or hesitant to provide you with answers to your questions, then find another breeder. Keep in mind that all breeders who are members of a kennel club are not necessarily reputable breeders. I have been contacted by many unsuspecting clients, over the years, who have been sold a puppy that is simply not up to breed standard or is of sub-standard quality. Understand that even though you may be getting a purebred dog, that fact in itself does not certify it to be a quality animal. Your intended veterinarian is also a valuable source of information when seeking a reputable source for your puppy.

Take your time and do your research thoroughly. You should, if at all possible, ask to see both the mother and the father of your puppy. By seeing both parents, you will be able to get a pretty good idea of the quality of the adult dogs and consequently a good indication of what your puppy may be like once he or she reaches maturity. Ask your breeder if she is able to provide you with the contact information of at least three customers who have purchased her puppies in the recent past. Go back a few years to see if this breeder has a consistent history of not only breeding good quality dogs but standing behind his or her dogs once they have been adopted into another family. Once you have your puppy home, it is often too late or very difficult to return it, especially if you or other family members have become attached to it.

If you are someone who really doesn't care if you have a purebred dog or not, I would recommend you seek out one or more animal rescue shelters in your area. There are plenty of very good puppies that end up in rescue shelters for any number of reasons. Most shelters are very careful in matching their rescued animals with potential adopters and will insist you do a trial match for a few days, or possibly even a week or more, before you are allowed to make the final adoption. Again, take your time and select your puppy carefully. This is a long-term commitment of many years, and you will want it to be a relationship that enhances you and your family's lives as well as your new puppy's life.

Bringing Your Puppy Home

The day has finally arrived that you will be bringing your new puppy home and begin to integrate her into your family.

Remember that new puppies are curious and mischievous by nature. There isn't much of anything they won't get into if you give them free range, so be vigilant. To make sure your puppy doesn't chew up your valuables, ingest, or play with things that could be hazardous to her health, keep the following in mind and prepare before your puppy arrives:

- Keep all electrical cords hidden and out of reach.

- Keep garbage bags off the floor or better yet inside a secure cabinet.

- Store cleaning and chemical products, and medicine up high, or in a locked cupboard.

- Don't leave children's toys lying around. Teach your children to put their toys away after use.

- Make sure all household plants in your dog's reach are not poisonous to dogs.

- Don't keep anything you deem valuable lying around within your dog's reach.

- Keep food trays off of low tables until your puppy has been taught boundaries. Some foods are toxic to dogs if ingested in sufficient quantities.

A good time to bring your puppy into your home is between seven and ten weeks of age. This is an ideal time to enrich the socialization process with humans. Most puppies at this age will also have had at least some of their shots, so they are at least partially protected against diseases. An excellent time to introduce your puppy into your home is just before the weekend or even better, if possible, at the beginning of a vacation period that you may choose to utilize as an opportune time to introduce your puppy to your family. Removing a puppy from its litter mates or former place of residence is in itself stressful. Do not add to this stress by bringing your puppy home during the holiday season or at a time when you may be expecting guests who may be visiting and staying over. Whatever time you choose to introduce your puppy to your family, make sure that everyone can meet the puppy in a relaxed environment. It is very important that young children are taught how to handle a puppy and to know when they must leave the puppy alone. If you already have existing family pets, such as a cat or another dog in your home, don't force the introduction and always provide supervision. Keep in mind that if you have an existing dog or cat, their noses will inform them that an intruder has arrived long before they actually meet or have visual contact. It is your responsibility to ensure that the initial meeting and any socialization between your new puppy and existing pets is carefully supervised and monitored. If you have any reason to suspect there might be a conflict, regardless of how slight, a good way to introduce your pets the first time is by having the puppy safely in a secure crate and allowing the other pet to sniff and meet the new arrival through the crate.

I do not recommend taking your puppy to areas such as dog parks or areas frequented by other dogs until your veterinarian has completed the vaccines and has indicated that your dog is old enough, is protected against most diseases, and can safely go to an off-leash park if you so desire. I personally do not recommend taking puppies to off-leash parks, though, and certainly not until the dog is at least six to eight months of age. Off-leash parks, though an okay concept, are also frequented by far too many inexperienced, irresponsible, and sometimes confrontational handlers and their out-of-control or unbalanced dogs.

Keep in mind that it is recommended that your puppy gets only minimal exercise during the first year of its life. This is particularly true if you have selected a large-breed dog that is growing rapidly. Forced exercise is never a good idea for puppies. Limit their exercise to a level and type they might experience if playing with puppies of their same age in a natural environment. Minimal exercise will allow adequate skeletal development to occur without undue stress.

Handling Your Puppy

It is very rare to find a person, young or old alike, that can resist the temptation to handle a puppy. People's desire to handle a puppy is a good thing; however, it is also important that when handling a puppy, it is done in a manner that is comforting and nonthreatening to the puppy. Remember that puppies by nature are not animals that would be picked up and carried around in another dog's arms. Of course, the mother dog may from time to time pick a puppy up by the scruff and gently move it from place to place; however, this is always short lived, and the puppy is carried much closer to the ground than a puppy would be when picked up by an adult, or even by most children.

To all of you who have a puppy at home now, or plan to get a puppy, you must be patient and consistent. Even when you pick your puppy up—which you surely will and should do—if he squirms and wiggles to get free at first, you must patiently hold him gently but firmly until he calms down, and only then should you gently praise him in a soothing tone of voice. Don't make the mistake of praising or attempting to soothe him while he is struggling to escape. Don't be afraid to handle your puppy. They are actually very resilient, and I always encourage new puppy owners to begin picking their puppy up right away. This does not mean that we should continuously be picking the puppy up and carrying him around; quite the opposite, actually. Do not constantly pick your puppy up. He has four good legs, so let him use them. The idea of picking him up is to get him used to the idea that you can and will handle him as you see fit, even when he may not particularly like it. I encourage all of my clients to pick their dog up periodically even as the dog grows into adulthood. The reason for this is so that the dog becomes accustomed to being picked up and feels safe in your arms in the event he becomes ill or is injured and you have to pick him up and carry him. This will greatly minimize the risk of the dog biting out of pain or fear, should he become injured or ill and have to be carried.

When you first get your puppy home, it is advisable to occasionally (once or twice per day) pick your puppy up and lay him safely on his back in your arms. Most puppies are quite resistant to this position; be patient as you gently but firmly restrain him and have him lie quietly on his back while you calmly talk to him until he calms down and relaxes. This gentle but firm process will go a long way toward establishing your respectful authority over the dog so that he will learn to accept and trust you to handle him. It is not advisable to allow children to handle your puppy in this way, though.

Children and Puppies

It is especially important to involve children in your puppy's upbringing, regardless of whether there are any children living in the home or not. You have both a responsibility to children in regards to your puppy and a responsibility to your puppy regarding the children.

Below are some things that every child should know about training puppies:

- Always use a gentle hand when handling the puppy.

- Do not disturb a sleeping puppy.

- Use a calm, quiet vocal tone with the puppy. No yelling or screaming.

- Never tease a puppy.

- Never allow the puppy access to children's toys. Many children's toys are made of a material that may be harmful to the puppy if ingested.

As a general rule of thumb, do not allow a child to handle a puppy without the supervision of an adult, and ensure that all children understand and adhere to all agreed upon rules of the household and lifestyle of the puppy.

It may also be appropriate to remind owners at this time that children do have a knack for winding up dogs: children move erratically, use high squeaky voices, and often play roughly and relentlessly. To avoid unwanted social behaviour later in your puppy's life, it is important to discourage children from playing tug-of-war with the puppy, playing chasing games, or engaging in other activities that potentially lead to detrimental behaviours. Consider that your puppy will likely start to view smaller children much like she might view another puppy, which will not only lead to leadership issues later in the relationship, but will also promote play bites, jumping, and playful mock attacks. Harmless as they may seem, play bites will not stop when the game stops and can quickly become a real life problem for the children and the puppies. In addition, teaching a puppy to be chased by children, in particular, may well have a negative impact on developing a reliable recall and overall obedience and behaviour management later in the dog's life.

If you want to include children in your puppy training process (and this is encouraged), teach the child how to enthusiastically encourage the puppy to come to them and to initiate play with the focus on praise or a toy instead of the child's flailing hands or feet. Having the puppy come to you, rather than you going to the puppy, helps to establish rank in the family and begins to instill the foundation for recall by teaching the puppy that going to the owner is always a rewarding experience.

If the puppy becomes reliant on being retrieved by her owner, she is less likely to pay attention (or even care where its owner is) once the puppy begins to mature mentally. A puppy that is a bit of an explorer and accustomed to having her owner follow her around will be more likely to wander off with little concern over getting lost or separated from her owner or pack leader.

Additionally, it is important to have the children participate in your puppy's feeding routine and early puppy training exercises. Having the children involved in feeding the puppy will also be beneficial in establishing the children's hierarchy within the family pack and will enable them to have fun teaching and instilling a few early command words such as "sit" and "stay."

Most children, like most puppies, have short attention spans. They may show a genuine desire to learn and partake in the obedience exercises for the puppy; however, without the guidance and support of the higher-ranking members of the household, all good intentions are liable to backfire for all involved. For children, I find it best to keep it simple and give them rules and responsibilities that are simple to follow and likely to (1) produce small but progressive victories for them and the puppy and (2) develop the children's confidence in later dog handling. A good place to start is to concentrate on having the child feed the dog and teach the dog to sit and wait for her food until told to "take it."

Crate Training

I find it interesting that there are so many dog owners who are reluctant or absolutely refuse to crate train their puppy. I am convinced these good people have not been exposed to proper information surrounding the many benefits of crate training their puppy, as well as the many benefits they will reap from taking the time to teach their puppy to sleep in a crate. After all, most of us have our own private room such as a bedroom when we need some peace and quiet, or simply need a quiet place to unwind from a hard day at work. Doesn't it just make sense to bestow on your puppy the same basic right? Let's start by remembering that puppies (*Canis lupus familiaris*) and all domestic dogs are considered a subspecies of the grey wolf (*Canis lupus*). As such, dogs have retained much of the wolf's natural den instincts (I tell you this only in the hope of helping you understand and accept that when used properly, crates are not "bad" or "cruel" in any way at all). Other animals that naturally use dens include foxes, cougars, coyotes, and of course bears, which hibernate in dens, although not necessarily to the extent some people would have you believe. Yes, dogs will seek shelter in the form of a den for warmth, protection, certainly for birthing, and often when they are sick or do not feel well. This does not mean that I believe in or support the practice of dogs being left in a crate for extended periods of time. A good rule of thumb may be to kennel your puppy for no longer than two hours at a time for each month of age, up to a maximum of eight hours—but only when there is no other option available. In fact, when properly utilized for training purposes, crates are often one of the most humane tools we have at our disposal to minimize the chances of a puppy getting into trouble for messing on your new carpet. Prevention can often be a whole lot better as a teaching tool than dealing with an accident after the fact, especially if you are not blessed with an abundance of patience.

For those of you who do choose to crate train a puppy, I suggest that first, you visit a reputable pet supply store with your dog. I always recommend purchasing a crate that will be suitable for your puppy once he has reached maturity. By making sure that the dimensions of your initial crate purchase are going to be appropriate for your puppy once he is full grown, you will only have to purchase one crate rather than two or more. If your puppy is a breed that is likely to grow into quite a large dog, then do your best to purchase a crate that will fit that particular breed at maturity. What you will have to do, though, is block part of the crate off so that the crate is just large enough for your puppy to walk into, turn around, and comfortably lay down inside. Regardless of the crate size you decide on, it is imperative that it be adjusted as your puppy grows so that it is no bigger than what is required for your puppy to walk into, turn around, and lay down comfortably. Many crates today come with panels that can easily be adjusted to provide more space inside of the crate to accommodate the puppy as he grows. Crates come in a variety of materials. Personally, I am a fan of good quality, "airline approved" plastic composite crates. These crates are sturdy, lightweight, and provide privacy for the puppy. One of the drawbacks of this type of crate, though, is that they do not fold down to a compact size when not in use as many of the wire mesh crates do. Wire mesh crates, in my opinion, tend to be less sturdy, offer little privacy, and are somewhat noisy as the dog moves around inside. They do offer the advantage of folding down to a very compact size for travel, and most are provided with detachable dividers that are easily adjusted to suit your puppy as he develops physically.

Once you have decided on the crate that best suits your lifestyle and is suitable for your breed of puppy, you can begin the crate training process. I find that a good way to first introduce your puppy to his new private room (crate) is to just place the crate in an area that is frequented by your puppy; however, before you do so, it is a good idea to take a soft blanket or bed that the puppy is already familiar with and place it inside the crate. Open the door wide and prop it open, or if you prefer you can remove the door completely at first. What you want to accomplish by doing this is to observe your puppy's initial reaction to this strange looking, and even stranger smelling, box sitting within his living area. Most puppies are really quite curious, and often by simply placing the crate in a spot that your puppy is accustomed to, you will be able to calmly monitor how your puppy responds to this new piece of furniture. If your puppy simply ignores the crate that is fine, but it is even better if he decides to explore the interior of the crate. If you notice that your puppy readily goes inside the crate, just observe and remain silent. Don't make a big deal of it. If you don't make a fuss, then in all likelihood your puppy won't either. The best time to place the new crate in your puppy's space is as soon after you bring your puppy home as possible. Ideally, you may have even purchased your crate before bringing your puppy home or on the same day. If you do this, your puppy will merely accept the crate as part of his new home.

Plastic Crate

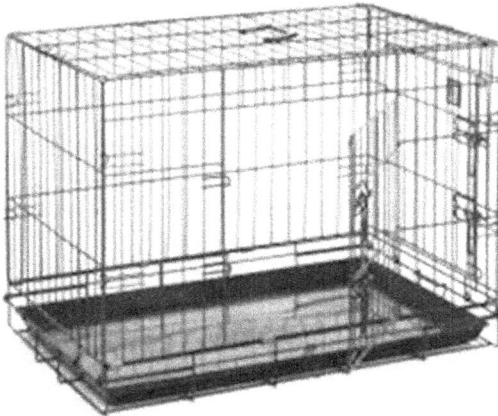

Wire Crate

Sleeping Arrangements
and Problem Sleepers

When it comes to sleeping quarters for your puppy, the options are practically infinite. However, it is my belief that there is one option that far supersedes any other sleeping quarter selection. I will always recommend a crate for the puppy right from the start. Regardless of what others may tell you, or sometimes even attempt to make you feel guilty about, crates are not cruel. Not in the least. Dogs are naturally den animals. That is to say that if they were left to provide their own accommodations, they would invariably seek out a hole (den) or another safe place in which to provide a home base, or a safe place to get out of the weather or take refuge in, should they feel threatened. Try to keep in mind that puppies sleep most of the time during the first few months of their life, so providing them with a nice snug crate (den) where they are safe and warm—a place of their very own where there are no intruders—is truly an act of kindness. I do, however, recommend that you give some careful consideration to the location you select for the crate when you first bring your puppy home (if you want to get some sleep that is).

When a puppy is first adopted by a human family, almost invariably that will also mean that the puppy is removed from all that is familiar to her, even though the puppy may be very happy to get into your vehicle and go home with you. Initially, the puppy will be the centre of attention, and everyone will be handling and playing with her, but sooner or later it will be time to retire for that first night in her new home. This is when she may decide she doesn't want to be alone in a place where the smells, sounds, sights, and even the temperature may be very different from what she has been accustomed to since the time she first came into the world. Don't be too surprised if this cute and cuddly little bundle of fur protests quite loudly when suddenly left alone in these new and somewhat frightening surroundings. To avoid a long and sleepless night, I recommend that for the first few nights your new puppy is in your home and settling in, you do all you can to ensure she feels safe and secure and of some importance so that you can get some sleep as well.

I recommend that the last thing you do before retiring for the night is to take your puppy out to your chosen potty area and take the time to ensure that she relieves herself just before retiring for the evening. Always take your puppy out for her potty break on a collar and a leash. This way, you will be able to subtly condition your puppy to go the bathroom in one area of your yard that you have selected for her and not become accustomed to using your whole yard as a lavatory. Although you may still have to get up once or even twice during the night to take her out, taking her out just before bedtime will eliminate at least one bathroom outing during the night.

One thing that I have always done when I first adopted a small puppy is to place her crate right at my bedside that first night. I will often take a sock or undershirt that I have worn and put it in the crate with her so that my smell is right there with her. By placing the crate right beside your bed and well within arm's reach, you can address her protesting without having to get out of bed in the event she begins to fuss during the night. If your puppy wakes you up in the night, it is always a good idea to check the clock to ensure that she is not really telling you that she does need to go out to the bathroom. A good rule of thumb is that a healthy puppy should be able to control her bladder for approximately two hours for each month of age, so if your puppy is two months old when you bring her home, she should be okay to sleep in her crate for approximately four hours before needing to go out. If only a short time has passed since retiring for the night and your puppy starts to raise a ruckus, then chances are it is not because she needs a bathroom break, but more likely that she simply wants company. If that is the case and the crate is right beside your bed, you can reach your hand out and sharply rap or slap the top of the crate with the flat of your hand as soon as she starts to cry or object to being confined. If you react quickly and effectively, and with sufficient force to ensure the noise of your hand slapping the crate is quite loud, the chances are good that your puppy will immediately stop her protesting. If you find it necessary to resort to this step, it is absolutely imperative that you do not utter a single sound. Most people have a really difficult time resisting the urge to say something negative to the puppy such as "no" or "quiet" or something to that effect. If you are one of these people, don't bother to slap the crate for it will not result in the desired outcome—to surprise the puppy into being quiet. Look at this from the puppy's point of view. She protests and the only consequence is an immediate and loud noise from outside her crate. She does not get any acknowledgement whatsoever from the human sleeping there beside her, perhaps the same person that had just been playing with her and being so kind a few short minutes or hours before. If you say anything, anything at all, then you have effectively rewarded the puppy for whining or barking in the first place. Keep in mind that the reason your puppy became vocal in the first place was to attract your attention. If you converse with her at all, even a single word, positive or negative, then you just gave the puppy exactly what she wanted. If you don't say a word and simply slap the crate, then her barking or protesting brings a loud and unexpected noise. In most cases, puppies won't repeat that mistake more than a few times, and the reason is that they quickly associate their protesting with bringing about that loud, impersonal, and daunting noise. What if, though, you have one of those more persistent puppies who does not take that loud noise seriously and continues to insist that you negotiate with her? Well now is the time you may have to progress to a slightly more intense approach. Here is what I would do in this case.

Before putting your puppy in her crate for the evening, and after making sure she has had ample opportunity to relieve herself, attach a short line to her collar. An old shoelace works very well and is light and long enough so that you are able to string it through the front of the crate (or side) and secure it in a way that the puppy cannot pull the line into the crate with her. Now, you will want to be sure that the end of the line is close enough to you so that you can quickly take hold of it the instant the puppy begins to protest about being in the crate, and give the line a sharp "pop". Remember that the puppy is attached to the other end of the line, so when she whines (protests) and you "pop" the line, the puppy will immediately be subjected to an abrupt (not hard) collar correction. If she whines again, repeat the process. I have never found a puppy that would continue protesting or complaining after just a few very short but sudden "mini consequences" for her actions. Think of it this way, the same way your puppy will perceive this response to her outburst: Seeing as you are not going to utter a single sound, she will not connect this slight correction to you. She will, however, quickly link the leash tweak to her whining. As soon as she whines she receives a sharp, short, correction. The moment she stops protesting, so do the corrections. Puppies, although just babies, are still very clever. She will immediately connect the whining with a correction and will almost instantly cease whining and will be fast asleep in no time. One more time, **do not talk to your puppy when applying this technique**. If you do, you will not obtain the results I have described. May I remind you again, you must have patience. Keep in mind that your new puppy is a baby, a baby that just had everything that was familiar to her taken away when she came home with you. I understand that you may be tired and want to sleep; however, developing your patience and understanding of your puppy now will forever pay dividends as you move forward with this life-long partnership.

Feeding Location

There is no one right or wrong place in your home that you must select as a feeding location for your puppy. Some locations certainly are more appropriate than others; however, where you decide to feed your puppy, and subsequently your adult dog, depends to a large extent upon the layout of your home and your feeding location preferences. There are a variety of factors, though, that I do encourage people to take into account whilst they are in the process of selecting the best feeding location for their newly arrived puppy.

Potentially undesirable feeding locations may include, but are not limited to:

a) near or in front of a busy doorway;

b) on or near a heating or cold air vent;

c) near a stereo or TV speaker;

d) in a busy hallway;

e) near the family's dining table (remember that the puppy will grow);

f) in an area of the home that is either too hot or too cold;

g) in the kitchen where he would be underfoot while preparing meals;

h) adjacent to another pet feeding location;

i) near another pet's litter box;

j) near household cleaning products; or

k) on your carpet (pick a location with a floor surface that is easy to clean up).

Please keep in mind that no one knows your home and the dynamics of your home better than you do; for that reason, the information included in this section is intended as a reference guide only. It may well be that you have already selected a location that is perfect for you, your puppy, and your family, even though I may not have mentioned it here.

Nutrition

No book on raising and shaping puppy behaviour would be complete without the inclusion of a basic nutrition section.

The author wishes to acknowledge Wendy and Jack Volhard for their kind and generous contribution to this section of this book. Canine nutrition is a widely debated topic and one that requires a great deal of knowledge to speak about intelligently. I have had the honour of meeting the well-known author, dog trainer, and world-famous canine nutrition expert Wendy Volhard on more than one occasion. It is with the utmost respect and appreciation that I acknowledge Wendy and Jack Volhard's contribution to this section. Wendy has graciously permitted me to include information from from one of her latest books, *Dog Training for Dummies 3rd edition* (2010). Wendy is also the coauthor of my favourite book written on canine nutrition, the *Holistic Guide for a Healthy Dog, Second Edition* (2000).

This section is not intended to turn you into an expert on canine nutrition but is designed to help you understand some basic concepts. First and foremost, it is important to realize that every dog has his own nutritional needs. Even though your first dog may have done perfectly well on a particular food, that same food may be completely unacceptable for your current puppy.

In this section, we guide you through the overwhelming task of trying to find the right food for your puppy. The information contained in this section—with particular thanks to Jack and Wendy Volhard—will work for the vast majority of dogs and is intended to save you from the nerve-racking task of walking blindly down endless pet food aisles, trying to make informed choices from the hundreds of foods offered. We will discuss your puppy's nutritional needs, show you how to find the right food to maintain your dog's health, and decipher how to interpret dog food labels. We will also include a brief overview on how your dog's digestive system functions. In recent years, the market has exploded with different types of pet food: Dry, freeze-dried, frozen raw, dehydrated, canned, semi-moist, and grain-free foods are available in a bewildering variety.

Evaluating Your Dog's Current Food

The following is a quick checklist that Wendy Volhard (Volhard and Volhard 2010, 65) has compiled to help dog owners determine if their dog is getting what he needs from the food they are feeding him. I find this quick checklist invaluable as a reference tool that can help you determine whether your dog is getting what he needs from his current food. This guide can come in handy at any time throughout your dog's life.

- He doesn't want to eat his food.

- He has large, voluminous stools that smell awful.

- He has gas.

- His teeth get dirty and brown.

- His breath smells foul.

- He burps a lot.

- He constantly sheds.

- He has a dull coat.

- He smells like a dog.
- He is prone to ear and skin infections.
- He has no energy or is hyperactive.
- He easily picks up fleas or ticks.
- He has to be frequently dewormed.

All of these conditions may occasionally crop up with any dog—but only occasionally. When several of the items on the list occur frequently or continuously, you need to find out why.

Nutritional Needs

The cliché "garbage in, garbage out" applies with terrifying validity when referring to pet nutrition. Like your body, your dog's body consists of cells—a lot of them. Each cell needs the following nutrients to function properly: protein, carbohydrates, fat, vitamins, minerals, and water.

In contrast to humans, puppies grow fast. During the first seven months of a puppy's life, his birth weight increases anywhere from fifteen to forty times, depending on his breed. For strength and proper growth to occur, he needs the right food. He also needs twice the amount of food as an adult while he is growing, especially during growth spurts. Nutritional deficiencies at an early age, even for short periods, can cause problems later on. The most critical period for a puppy is between two and seven months, which is the time of maximum growth. Puppy foods contain more protein than adult or maintenance foods. Manufacturers know that puppies need more protein for growth. Nonetheless, you need to know the source of the protein; that is, whether it is animal or plant-based protein. By law, the heaviest and largest amount of whatever ingredient contained in the food has to be listed first. By looking at the list of ingredients, you can easily discover the protein's origin. For example, if the first five ingredients listed come from four grains, the majority of the protein in that food comes from grains. The more grains in a dog food, the cheaper it is to produce.

If you choose carefully, you can select a food that is suitable for a growing puppy as well as for an adult dog. Look for food that has two or three animal proteins in the first five ingredients—or better yet, one that lists animal proteins as its first two or three ingredients. Check out foods that are listed for all growth stages or that are specifically designed for puppies.

Digestion Information

In a study done on gastric emptying time by the American Animal Hospital in 1992, it was found that raw, frozen, and dehydrated raw foods pass through a dog's stomach and into the intestinal tract in 4½ hours. After that time span, the dog is already receiving energy from that food. We recommend these diets, especially for performance dogs, because they're the most easily digested.

Semi-moist foods—canned food, the hamburger-shaped kind that you find in boxes on the supermarket shelf, and the ones in rolls like sausages take almost nine hours to pass through the stomach.

Dry foods take between 15 and 16 hours to digest, so if you choose to feed Buddy any kind of dry processed dog food, it will be in his stomach from morning until night. This slow digestion isn't important for the average pet, but if you work or show your dog or want him to live a long life, it becomes important. You don't ever want to work or jump Buddy when his stomach is full of food, nor do you want him to die prematurely.

The above insert is from Volhard and Volhard (2010, 75)

House Training

House training is certainly one of the most varied subjects when it comes to a puppy's primary education. Like almost everything in life, there is no "one way" to house train a puppy. There is a wide variety of house training methods and techniques in circulation; however, there is one approach that is so superior to all other methods I will only discuss this one process. The method I am going to describe for you is commonly referred to as crate training. Now before we get started and before you become concerned that your dog may develop a distaste for her crate should you use this method, please allow me to assure you that I have never seen a properly crate-trained puppy dislike her crate in any way. Quite the contrary, puppies actually develop a fondness for their crate and will often go there on their own when they want some privacy or just want to feel warm and safe.

When I speak of training a dog of any age, be it a puppy or a mature animal, I want to impress upon you once again that frustration or anger has absolutely no place in a dog's education. If you are frustrated or angry, you simply cannot teach. So even though your puppy may do what all puppies do (pee or poop on your floor), you must maintain the role of a good teacher, and good teachers will coach without any trace of anger or frustration clouding their teaching (leadership) skills.

In order to teach a puppy that it is not acceptable to relieve herself inside your home (not hers), you must begin immediately to prepare her not only for where it is acceptable to relieve herself, but more importantly where it is not acceptable to go, and that includes anywhere in your home. Let's get started.

Regardless of how vigilant you may be, invariably sooner or later your puppy is going to make a mess somewhere inside your home. Puppies don't know that it is not acceptable to do so. This is where you come in. Your responsibility is to teach your puppy where it is acceptable to relieve herself and where it is not. Don't be one of those people who are misled into believing that you have to "catch her in the act," because that may be harder to do than you might think. Puppies are quick; they can squat and pee and be on their way before we even realize anything has happened.

Although puppies can't see or hear at birth, their sense of smell is available to them right from birth; therefore, at seven or eight weeks of age (the age they are ready to be adopted) their sense of smell is quite keen. Even if you don't catch your puppy in the act of messing on the floor, not to worry: once you take her back to that spot, her nose will tell her exactly what it is.

Four simple steps to house training your puppy.

If your puppy has peed or pooped in your home, it is your responsibility to assume the role of a good teacher (leader). Keep in mind that a puppy does not understand that it is not acceptable to relieve herself inside your home (yes your home, not hers; that is a whole article in itself and not one that needs to be discussed in this book), then you will need to provide a mild negative consequence for doing so. Whether you caught your puppy in the act or not is somewhat irrelevant at this point, as you will soon see. A puppy's nose works just fine; therefore, whether you catch her in the act or not is of little significance. She knows the smell of her own urine or excrement. Before we continue, though, I must stress that **I do not endorse** or condone in any way the act of rubbing your dog's nose in her excrement. To do so is overkill, and will serve only to show your puppy the ultimate disrespect. Remember that training a dog, puppy or otherwise, is largely dependent upon forming a bond between you and your puppy. This relationship must be built on the foundation of trust and respect. I am sure you will agree that rubbing a dog's nose in her own waste is not showing her any respect whatsoever. Teach—don't humiliate!

What is crate training?

Crate training can be an efficient and effective way to house train a puppy. Puppies naturally do not like to soil their resting/sleeping quarters if given adequate opportunity to eliminate elsewhere. Temporarily confining your puppy to a small area such as her crate will drastically reduce your puppy's tendency to urinate or defecate. However, there is still a far more important aspect of crate training. If your puppy fails to eliminate while she is confined, then it should go without saying she will need to eliminate immediately when she is released. Once she is released and taken to the area you have chosen, and has eliminated in your presence, you now have created an opportunity to reward and praise her for going to the bathroom in an approved location.

Crate training is one of the most efficient and effective ways to train a puppy.

The single most important aspect of puppy training is that you reward and praise your puppy each and every time she does the right thing. Conversely, you must provide a mild negative consequence when she does anything that is undesirable. For example, praise her when she eliminates outside instead of in the house. The more time you spend with your puppy, the quicker and easier it will be to train her.

The key to house training is to establish a routine that (1) increases the chances your puppy will eliminate in the right place in your presence so that she can be praised and rewarded, and (2) decreases the likelihood that your puppy will eliminate in the wrong place so that she will not develop habits that are much harder to break later on.

It is important that you make provisions for your puppy when you are not home. Until your puppy is house trained, she should not be allowed the free run of your house. Otherwise, she will develop a habit of leaving piles and puddles anywhere and everywhere. Don't be fooled into thinking that you can confine her to a small area such as a kitchen, bathroom, or utility room that has water and/or stain resistant floors and that she will learn not to mess in the house. Actually, even though such confinement may make it easier to clean up her mess, you are still creating an environment that condones messing within your home. Confinement is not crate training!

Step 1: Connecting the dots (making sure she understands what it is you are disciplining her for). In the event that your puppy messes in your home, which invariably all puppies do sooner or later, she has presented you with an opportunity to provide not only education surrounding the rules about messing in your home, but also an opportunity to demonstrate your steadfastness as a strong, firm, and fair pack leader. To do so effectively will require that you are able to control your emotions and remain calm but assertive throughout the duration of this teaching opportunity. Allowing anger or frustration to creep into this critical teaching step will serve no useful purpose and, in fact, will most likely serve only to frighten and confuse your puppy. Any great teacher will understand that teaching requires patience. Patience and resolve are powerful tools during the constructive education of your puppy and will serve to cement the bond between you and your puppy for years to come. Teaching a puppy (or a human for that matter) requires a balanced approach. In the education of a puppy, not only is positive reinforcement a necessary ingredient in the puppy's education, but discipline (not punishment) is equally important. Far too many well-intentioned new dog owners are derailed by those who spout that "positive reinforcement only" is the road to success with a puppy. If we stop and think about that illogical approach for even a few seconds, we will quickly realize that it just does not make a whole lot of sense. How can you positively reward a negative behaviour and expect that action to cease?

Step 2: Discipline. Let's imagine for a moment that your puppy is like almost every other puppy and she has messed in your house. If that is the case, then your puppy has provided you with an opportunity to teach, and teach you must. Don't be fooled into believing that it is imperative that you actually catch your puppy in the act of soiling your floor. Even though the ideal situation might be that you actually catch your puppy in the act, I have determined over the almost forty years that I have been working with and studying dogs that if we conduct ourselves appropriately, it is as effective to seize the opportunity to teach some time after the fact as it is if you catch your puppy in the act. *This delayed teaching does not apply to all behaviours. For now, I ask that you only attempt to discipline after the fact in the cases where going to the bathroom in your home is involved.* Attempting to discipline for most behaviours after the fact is almost always unproductive and often very confusing to your puppy. The reasons it is not imperative that you discipline for messing in the house immediately after the act are that (a) most often you won't actually see her do it, and (b) the puppy's nose will allow her to associate your ethical teaching with the mess on the floor. All right, so you have discovered that your puppy has urinated on your floor. What you need to do (if you didn't see her do it) is to get your puppy and take her back to the spot where she has urinated. Now, it is imperative that throughout this teaching exercise you remain calm yet assertive. This is a tremendous opportunity for you to practice being an excellent teacher and thus a great leader. This is not a time where you can afford to allow anger or frustration to invade your mental state. This is a "teaching moment"! Take your puppy back to the location of the urine and close enough to it so that you are absolutely confident she can smell it. *Do not rub* her nose in it! To do so would be unnecessary, unproductive, and disrespectful to the puppy.

Showing him his mess.

Once you are certain your puppy has been able to smell her own urine, then you must begin to speak to her in a firm voice (connecting the dots). It is inconsequential what you say, but it is important how you speak to her. You must talk in a very firm, loud (not shouting) tone of voice. You want your puppy to associate your firmness with that mess there on the floor or in the carpet in front of her. Once you have shown your puppy her mess and held her close to it while speaking firmly to her, turn her away from her mess, take her face in your hands, and gently shake her while you continue to lecture her. This firm (not rough) discipline simulates what a mother dog might do. While you have your puppy's face cupped in your hands and as you are scolding her, you must make her look directly into your eyes. This is one of those times when eye contact is necessary. You want your puppy to realize and understand that it is her that you are directing your discipline towards. If after a few seconds of scolding, your puppy turns her eyes away so as to not look into your eyes, then turn her head (you took control of her head when you cupped her face in your hands) so that she must look into your eyes as you continue to scold her. If she tries to wiggle free or screams like you are killing her, do not be dissuaded. You are not hurting her, and she will quickly learn that all the shrieking in the world is not going to cause you to release her. You are teaching at this point in time, and she is not going to be allowed to persuade you otherwise. Now, continue to gently shake and scold her for approximately one minute. Yes, that is a long time for sure. You need to make an impression on your puppy, and that impression will be that you do not tolerate her messing in *your* den (home). Then, following approximately one minute of firm but fair discipline comes the most important part of all, isolation.

Gently shaking and reproaching.

Step 3: Isolate. Following the stern but fair discipline described in step 2, it is important that you now give your puppy time to absorb what just happened. To do this, the most efficient method is to isolate the dog from all others, including people. Although some people might be tempted to allow sympathy to creep into this process, you must not allow that to happen if you hope to be effective. The puppy does not want you to feel sorry for her. You haven't done anything wrong. You have simply engaged in a teaching exercise. Now that you have associated her mess on the floor with a negative consequence (scolding and gentle shaking), you are going to take her learning a step further. You are now going to (at least in the puppy's mind) evict her from your pack. This is a crucial step in the teaching process. To do this, following the verbal scolding you will simply take the puppy to her crate, place her inside, close the door, and walk away. There is no need to scold her further; in fact, to do so would be counterproductive. You are now going to let her mind do the rest. By placing her in her crate and closing the door, you have restricted the puppy's movements. Once she is in her crate, you must not communicate with her in any way. Don't allow anyone else to communicate with her either. If you have another puppy or even another pet in the house, you must make sure they do not have access to her crate area. What you have done is effectively removed your puppy from your pack. By placing her in her crate, although it is warm, safe, and secure, you have limited her ability to go seek companionship from any other person or pet. Because dogs are pack animals, her instincts will take effect and lead your puppy to believe she is now all alone in the world. Pack animals form packs for survival reasons, so if your puppy has no pack, her very survival is threatened. Let her think about this for approximately thirty to forty-five minutes and up to one hour if your puppy is approaching six months of age. Yes, this is a form of teaching, and no, she will not learn to dislike his crate. The crate is simply a confinement tool to prevent her from forming a pack with anyone or anything else and to compel her to think about what brought this situation on in the first place. She will quickly begin to understand that it is the act of messing in your territory that caused her to be expelled from your pack. Oh, one more thing: If your puppy responds with howls of protest when you place her in her crate, then you must take action. Whatever you do, do not respond by verbally scolding her. If you howl when she howls, all you will get is you and her making a whole lot of noise together, and neither of you will win. If this happens, casually return to her crate and with the flat of your hand "whack" the top of the crate so as to create a booming noise inside the crate.

You must not look at her, talk to her, or touch her when you go back to whack the crate. Simply smack the crate and walk away. You may have to do this a few times; however, be persistent. It will take only minutes for your puppy to learn that all she is going to gain from making a fuss when you confine her is a loud noise, not from you but as a direct result of her protests.

Step 4: Reward. Following approximately thirty to sixty minutes of total confinement (depending on the puppy's age), you will return to your puppy's crate, open the door, and gently take the puppy outside to the area you have chosen for her to use as her bathroom area. It is now imperative that you remain with your puppy until she goes to the bathroom so that you can praise her enthusiastically for doing so. (Make sure you enthusiastically celebrate her eliminating outside, or in the area you have chosen.) Your puppy must learn that this is an excellent thing to do. Now as you can see, messing in the house was a negative experience and going to the bathroom outside became a very positive experience. If that makes sense to you, then you can be assured it makes sense to your puppy as well. This method of house training has proven to be so effective I rarely even discuss other methods, for there is no other method of house training that is as fair and efficient as the one just described.

Leaving Your Puppy Home Alone

One of the top canine behaviour dilemmas new puppy owners are faced with shortly after they bring their puppy home is the difficulty of leaving their puppy at home, or even by itself in another room, even for a few minutes. Beware! If you are one of these people, you are setting you and your puppy up for substantial tribulations later on; in fact, these issues will not take long to begin to surface. Don't allow anyone to convince you that a puppy that is left alone and throws a tantrum suffers from what is now being referred to as "separation anxiety." Call it what it is, and that is a *behavioural problem*. There may be cases of separation anxiety that exist; however, they are few and far between. How do I know this? Well, because I am called upon to deal with this alleged separation anxiety over and over again, and I can assure you that when it is addressed as a behavioural issue, it is relatively easy to correct. Puppies by their very nature are hard-wired to be left alone right from birth and are quite comfortable with it. What obstructs this primal instinct is our human propensity to go against what is natural to the puppy. It is absolutely normal for wild animals such as wolves, foxes, coyotes, and many others to go off in search of food and leave their pups in the den. They are taught from birth that this is a natural phenomenon and as such are quite accepting of it.

If you take the time to teach your puppy that leaving him alone is a normal process, then not only will you be teaching your puppy a valuable life lesson, but you will be doing both you and your puppy a huge favour. Nobody wants a puppy that shrieks and howls when it is left unaccompanied, including your neighbours. Being a considerate dog owner as well as a good neighbour requires that you or your puppy do not unreasonably disturb your neighbour. There is absolutely no need for your puppy to turn out to be a noisy neighbour.

One of the first steps in teaching your puppy that it is routine for you to leave him alone for short periods of time must begin immediately after bringing your puppy home. Just like you occasionally want and need some private time, your puppy does as well. Take advantage of your puppy's natural desire to rest to assist you in teaching your puppy to be content and confident when left alone. This is where your crate training will pay huge dividends in another way other than just in toilet training. Remember to remain calm and relaxed while you are preparing your puppy to become confident and comfortable, even when you have to leave him alone. This is a natural occurrence, so when preparing your puppy to remain alone for short periods of time, it is equally important that you stay calm and relaxed (*balanced*) as well.

Begin by leaving your puppy by himself for just a minute or less at a time. Place him gently in his crate, praise him enthusiastically for going into the crate, and then exit the room. Stay out of the room for only a few seconds to start with. If your puppy remains quiet, re-enter the room but do not pay any attention to him. Move around a bit and then leave the room again for a few more seconds. If when entering the room you notice out of the corner of your eye that your puppy is napping, move around a bit and exit the room once again for a few minutes or until you hear your puppy stirring but not yet making a fuss. Re-enter the room without paying any attention to the puppy, and move around a bit before going to the puppy's crate. Calmly open the crate and without further ado gently pick the puppy up and take him out for a bathroom break. Once he has gone to the bathroom outside, weather permitting, you may want to allow your puppy to roam around outside for a short time so that he gets to use that marvelous nose of his to explore and take advantage of all the adventures the outdoors has to offer. Make this outdoor play time fun for your puppy, so don't subject him to a lot of commands at this stage. Let your puppy be a puppy. There is plenty of time for training a little later on in his life.

When you bring your puppy back inside, you can play with him inside for a bit. If you have limited time and can't watch him, then his crate is a good place for him to be. Remember that dogs are den animals, and as such his crate should be viewed as nothing more than a warm, safe, and secure shelter. This is a place where your puppy can go when he is tired or just wants to feel safe and secure. Teaching your dog at an early age that his crate is a place of comfort and safety is very important and will not only serve you well over the many years to come, but will also serve your dog's instinctive needs in a positive way. Be sure not to over stimulate your puppy prior to putting him in his crate. Gently teach him that when you tell him to "go to your crate," it is not a request but a gentle command and that his crate will always be a place he can go to be comfortable and secure. Don't be fooled into believing that it is only you who needs the occasional break from your puppy; just as often your puppy will want a break from you!

Now that you are in the process of teaching your puppy that it is customary for you to leave him alone while you are home, you can also begin to expose him to being left alone when you have to go out of the home. In preparation for this next step, one thing I should mention is that you do want to ensure your puppy is comfortable whenever he is required to stay in his crate. A cozy blanket, or even a small dog bed designed to fit inside his crate, is always a good option, providing, of course, that your puppy isn't one of those puppies that feels his bed or blanket is meant to be devoured. It is equally important that you do not wash or clean his bedding too often. Dogs do not appreciate the potent fragrance of most laundry detergents or fabric softeners. Of course, you wouldn't want to have your dog sleeping on a dirty blanket or pad in his crate, but being too clean is just as appalling as being too dirty. A good idea is to wash his bedding in a mild unscented detergent and then let it air-dry outside where it is exposed to the fresh air for several hours before placing it in his crate.

Now that you have been practicing telling your puppy to "go to your crate" and then placing your puppy in his crate in preparation for actually leaving him alone when you go out, you can initiate the next part of this step. Practice picking up your keys, putting on your cap, jacket, and your shoes, and even picking up your purse (or wallet), so as to get your puppy habituated to these human actions and they become part of his regular routine (just as going into his crate is a standard practice) and are not perceived as clues that he is about to be left alone. All of this groundwork preparation is designed to create a positive association with his crate; to get him used to going there voluntarily when there is nothing happening around your home; and to get him to realize that spending time in his crate is not only positive, but a part of your household's regular routine, just as leaving him in his crate in another room while you are home is a natural occurrence.

Once you have had the opportunity to run through having your puppy go into his crate several times each day at irregular intervals and leaving him alone for several minutes at a time without incident, you are now ready to introduce the next step, and that is to actually leave your puppy alone at home. If you have followed the instructions outlined in this chapter (you have varied your routine and got your puppy comfortable with you picking up your keys and putting your shoes and jacket on without him reacting), you are now well prepared to advance to the next level. Be sure you do not change your regular routine in any way—and certainly do not over stimulate or under stimulate your puppy (one is as bad as the other)—just before leaving your home. Merely go about your everyday routine, and then just before leaving tell your puppy to "go to your crate," as you have done so many times before. Once your puppy is comfortable in his crate, and you have praised him for confidently entering his crate, simply turn and leave as if nothing has changed, for, in fact, it hasn't up to this point. The only difference is that this time you will actually leave your home. Try to introduce this first step of leaving your home at a time when you only have to leave for a few minutes, such as walking to the mail box to get the mail. As you leave, listen carefully for any signs of your puppy beginning to fuss about you leaving. If all is well, then quietly walk far enough away that your puppy will be convinced that you have vacated the premises, but not so far that you are unable to hear your puppy should he start to bark, whine, or throw a fuss of any kind. If your puppy remains silent and you feel it appropriate, you might even start your car, open the garage, back out and shut the garage door, and drive around the block. All of this should not take much more than five minutes. If all is quiet when you come back and approach the door into your home (or enter the garage and turn your car off), then you have been successful and so has your puppy. Proceed into the house as if nothing is out of the ordinary (in fact it is not), and when you are ready go to your puppy, open the crate door, and take him out for a bathroom break if you feel it is necessary. If not, then just allow him to follow you around your house or do his own thing until it is time to take him out for a regular bathroom break. Play with him before coming in and returning him to his crate for a few minutes. Throughout this introduction period of leaving your dog home alone, you must remain calm and exercise patience. Remember that training your puppy is meant to be an enjoyable experience and is as much for your puppy's benefit as it is yours, so relax and enjoy the experience.

Snatching Food Without Approval (Establishing Pack Order)

One of the most important rules of etiquette that you will want to instill in your puppy at an early age is that it is not acceptable for your puppy to pilfer food from anyone's hand, at any time, without first getting approval from the person holding the food. Equally crucial is that you establish with your puppy at an early age, that any food or article left on a countertop or table is never to be taken, whether it is from a low table or a full-height dining table. It is my belief that if every dog owner took the time to teach their dog, young or old, just this one fundamental rule, then dog bite incidents would be reduced by at least fifty percent. A dog that feels it has the right to snatch food from a person's hand, especially a child's hand, is much more likely to develop food aggression later in life. Many alleged dog bites are, in actuality, accidental bites due to a dog being disrespectful and snatching food from someone's hand, particularly from the hand of a toddler or young child. There is absolutely no excuse for not teaching a dog its proper position within the human pack. Your dog must learn to respect people of all ages so that he would never consider stealing from them. If we examine how a natural pack functions in nature, we will quickly appreciate that there is a definitive and respectful pecking order within the pack, with the strongest and wisest member assuming the lead position and the rest of the members assuming their rightful positions within the pack. Never would a juvenile dog consider stealing a meal from the leader while it was eating. If he were foolish enough to try, it would only happen once, and the young dog would be swiftly taught to respect both the leader of the pack and all other members that outranked the juvenile. Being that dogs are hard-wired with natural pack survival instincts right from birth, it is instinctive for them to wait for the higher members of the pack to eat first; the lower ranking members will eat once those who outrank them are finished. This same principle must be taught and applied within your family pack. Don't fret over your dog not liking you for establishing a well-defined hierarchy within your family pack. Quite the contrary, your puppy will respect you for doing so, as a dog does not really care where in the pack they fit, so long as they are taught to recognize their rightful position. One of the most overlooked needs of a dog is structure. So many well-meaning people spend far too much time worrying about providing their dog with an infinite supply of toys and treats (most of which are poorly constructed or are detrimental to their puppy's health); consequently, they overlook what a puppy really needs—structure. Your young puppy's primal instincts dictate that in order for him to survive, he must live in a structured environment. It is your responsibility to provide your puppy with an organized lifestyle: one in which he knows where he fits and can thrive and develop without the stress of wondering where he belongs. Remember that because dogs need structure in their life, if you don't provide your puppy with the stability he needs, it won't be long until he begins to establish his very own version of order, and his interpretation is often not all that palatable to us humans.

So, how do we teach a puppy never to steal food from a person's hands? Surprisingly enough it is so simple that it is almost embarrassing.

Keeping in mind that all training is to be done without any negative emotions whatsoever and that dogs of all ages learn by association, you are now ready to begin teaching your puppy to respect you and other humans so that your puppy will learn it is never permissible to take food from the hand of a human without first being told that it is okay to do so. You will also learn how to teach your puppy that any food or items of any kind that are located on a coffee table, dining room table, kitchen counter, or any place other than his normal eating area are out of bounds, and as such are not to be touched. Dogs have four natural primal instincts (fight, flight, avoid, and submit) that they are born with and that they instinctually rely on to survive. When teaching this exercise, you will quickly see one of those behavioural instincts (avoidance) come into play. What makes this task so easy to teach is that your puppy will immediately draw on his natural subconscious instincts in order to learn.

Let's get started. Seeing as you know your puppy better than anyone, you will also know what his favourite snack is. For the purpose of this exercise, I recommend choosing a human food such as a small piece of cheese, sausage, or anything else that you eat and that your puppy is likely to want to take from you. Now that you have selected your food of choice, it is time to commence teaching. If you follow the instructions below, it should only take a minute or so to teach your puppy that whatever is in your hand is not for him to steal from you and that he must show you the same respect he might show a mature dog and patiently wait without even looking at the food until such time you give him the approval to do so. With food in hand and your puppy on a light leash and collar, position your hand with the food in it right in front of the dog's nose and about two to four inches away—far enough away that your puppy would have to make a deliberate attempt to get the food. It is of the utmost importance that when you are teaching this exercise that (a) you do not say a word to your dog or make a single sound, and (b) that you do not pull your hand away from the dog as he reaches for the food. It is a good idea to kneel on the leash so that your puppy cannot wander off during this exercise. Be sure not to have the leash tight, but you will be kneeling on it so that in the event he decides to become distracted with other things he cannot simply run off and play elsewhere. Now that you are kneeling on the leash, hold the food in your nondominant hand in front of his nose, keeping your dominant hand free to issue the mild correction.

Light two finger tap under chin.

As your puppy reaches for the tasty treat you have in your hand, without making a sound, use your dominant hand to come up under his chin with your middle and index finger and give him a tap under the chin. The reason for coming up under his chin is so that your puppy will not see the movement. The reason we do not say anything to him is so that he does not associate the tap under the chin with us but rather to his act of reaching for, or attempting to take, something away from his leader. Remember that you ALWAYS want to remain a positive figure in your dog's eyes; therefore, if you never say anything negative to your puppy, he will never associate you with being negative. From your puppy's point of view, his entire attention, his sense of smell, as well as his eyes were focused entirely on the food. At that point, nothing existed in your puppy's mind except for that tempting smell and sight of that wonderful-smelling food. Just as he goes to reach for the food, something nips him under the chin. In his mind, it couldn't have been you because as soon as you tapped him under the chin and he aborted his reach for the food you praised him. If he repeats the act of reaching for the food, you will repeat the very same actions. Tap him under the chin, and as soon as he abandons his attempt to take the food you praise him with verbal and physical positive reinforcement. If after three repetitions of this process, your puppy continues to try to take the food from your hand, you may have to increase the intensity of the tap under the chin until it is of sufficient force that your puppy aborts his efforts to steal food from his leader, you! If done correctly, your puppy will almost instantly abort any attempts to steal food from a human; in fact, it is an extremely rare puppy that cannot be convinced within just a minute or maybe two minutes to stop all efforts to take food from your hand.

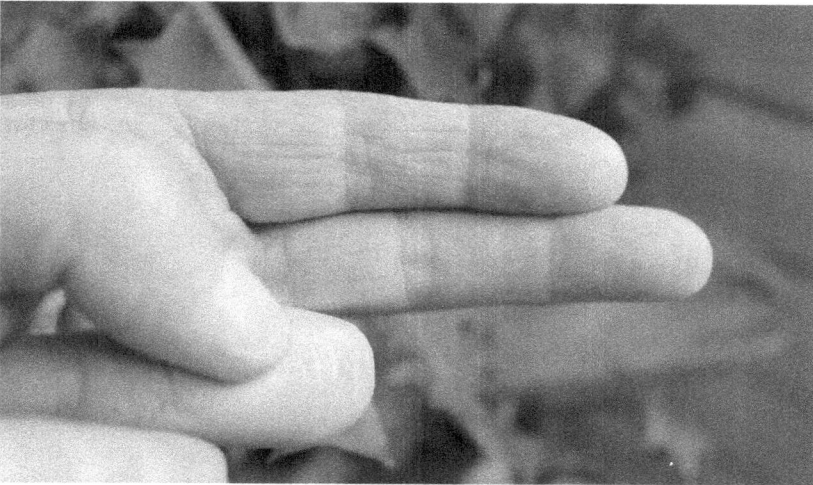

Light two finger tap under chin.

If you have a young child that you want the dog to learn to respect in the same way, you must do the teaching with the child present. Once your puppy exhibits an aversion to whatever is in your hand, then and only then have your child hold the food in front of the dog's nose and if necessary you will take the corrective action. Do not have the child attempt to teach the dog this exercise.

Now that you have successfully taught your puppy that you are a kind but firm leader (a leader to be respected and trusted) and that attempting to take food from your hand without your prior approval brings with it a negative consequence, you are now ready to teach you puppy not to touch food or even articles that have been placed on a table, even if that table happens to be at the perfect height for him to see and smell. You may notice that teaching this exercise is actually quite similar in many ways to teaching your puppy to respect boundaries, which are explained a bit further on in this book.

As in all exercises, you must be sure to have your puppy's collar on with a light leash attached before you attempt to teach your puppy this lesson. It is always a good idea to have set out the food you are using as "bait" prior to bringing your puppy into the room. Now that you have set out a tempting plate that may contain cheese, a bit of sausage, or any other mouth watering food that your puppy is going to smell and will be tempted to sample a taste, you can begin. Since you have your puppy on a collar and leash, let him find the food on his own (you may subtly guide him towards it if necessary) and even allow him to go close enough to smell it from a few inches away. Do not let him get close enough actually to take it. Now that he is close to the food and is exhibiting a desire to eat the food, this is where you begin the teaching process.

Keeping him a few inches away from the food, you are going to connect the dots, just as you did when teaching house training. Keeping him just out of range of the food on the table, you will point to the food, and in a firm voice, you will tell him in no uncertain terms that this food is not for him and that as such it is out of bounds. You must speak sternly while at the same time remaining calm and relaxed emotionally so that there is absolutely no negative emotion radiating from you. Remember you are now in teaching mode and you cannot teach if you are unbalanced emotionally in any way. You must be stern, but kind and relaxed at the same time. Now as you are keeping your puppy just out of range of the food, and speaking to him in a stern voice, you will also point to the food so that there is little doubt that the puppy knows that whatever you are talking about it certainly has something to do with the food there on the plate on the table in front of him. I am sure that at this point puppies must think we have lost our mind and are simply making noise. That is okay as in a few moments we will begin to teach the puppy the reasoning behind our speaking to this food. Now loosen your leash just enough so that the puppy can reach out towards the food. The moment he makes the slightest movement, give the leash a sharp "pop" back and away from the food so that as the puppy reaches for the food he gets a sharp little "pop" on his collar. You will immediately turn him away from the food, and as you do you must heap physical and verbal rewards on him so that he is amply rewarded for abandoning the food on the table. Now walk your puppy around the room while you are telling him just how wonderful he is, and after maybe a half to three-quarters of a minute stop the praise and lead him back in the direction of the food. As you approach the food, if your puppy begins to turn his head away so as not to even look at the food or he braces his front feet as if to say "I don't want to go near that food," then you must once again beginning enthusiastically praising him as you turn him away from the food. Repeat this process as many times as is required to get him to resist moving towards the food three times in a row. As soon as he has indicated three times in a row that he wants no part of the food on the table, end the training session. Remove the puppy from the room, and once he has been removed, return and remove the food, saving it for another training session the following day. The next day you will repeat this process, perhaps placing the food in another location. If you perform this exercise with a variety of food in a variety of different locations throughout your home over the course of the next seven days, you will have imprinted on your dog's brain that any time he sees food sitting around it is a really bad idea to even go near it. To ensure you are successful with this exercise, you must always remain positive and allow your puppy to learn. There is no place for negativism, frustration, or anger while you are teaching your puppy. If you allow any of these emotions to creep into your training, put your puppy away and wait until you are once again calm and relaxed before attempting to teach him further. A good rule of thumb to live by when you are teaching a puppy (or an older dog) is that if you are attempting to rid your dog of undesirable behaviour, you must say nothing negative. If you want to implant a desirable behaviour, then you must praise the heck out of him. Any negative words or emotions coming from you will only serve to teach your puppy that you are negative; as such, he will not learn to respect you and in some cases may even become afraid of you. Stay away from the commonly used word "NO." It is negative, and furthermore it just does not produce any positive results!

Socialization

Proper and adequate socialization is a subject I get asked about perhaps as much as or more than any other dog-related issue. It seems there is a belief out there that the lack of socialization is the root of most dog behaviour problems that arise later in a dog's life. It is common for me to be contacted by a client who is feeling guilty because their dog is showing aggression towards other dogs or sometimes even other humans, and they have been told by someone that this behaviour is due to the dog not being socialized enough when it was a puppy. I tend to disagree with this conclusion. Although I do believe that socialization is important in shaping a dog's character, I think that proper socialization is far more important. Socializing your puppy with the wrong dogs or people, or in the wrong environment, in my mind is much more detrimental than no socialization at all. Dogs by nature are very social creatures. They have to be in order to live in their natural pack environment. I believe that socializing your puppy has to be given careful consideration if you hope to avoid creating a negative experience for your puppy and consequently for you.

What I prefer to recommend for puppy socialization is that you restrict the puppy's exposure to close family and friends for the first two to three weeks (14 – 21 days) after bringing the puppy home. This will allow the puppy enough time to acclimatize to his new home and also let the puppy's "real self" begin to reveal itself. When you first bring a new puppy into your home, it is critical that you understand that your puppy will require some time to adjust to his new home and therefore will not necessarily be completely comfortable in his new environment for the first two to three weeks. This is the "honeymoon period," so to speak. Almost always by the second or third week, you will be seeing your puppy's real character emerging, and by then you will also have a pretty good idea of what to expect from him. Now is the time you might consider expanding his socialization circle, but do not take him to outside areas where other dogs frequent. The risk of contracting diseases is always present, particularly prior to the puppy being fully immunized. Your veterinarian is always a great source of advice on how, when, and where to socialize your puppy during the first four to six months of his life or until he is fully immunized. If you have one or two friends who have dogs that you know are friendly towards puppies and that are current on their vaccinations, then that is a great place to begin introducing your puppy to unfamiliar territory, new people, and other dogs. I recommend this approach because you not only know and trust the person who owns the dog you will be introducing your puppy to, but you will also be around a dog that you can trust to teach the puppy some dog etiquette without hurting it. You are also in a better position to control who and how people and dogs interact with your puppy. A bad experience at this tender age can mar your puppy for months to come. I have my own opinion on dog parks and puppy daycare, which I will discuss later. However, I strongly advise that you not allow anyone to talk you into taking your puppy to either of these locations until he is at least six months of age. The key to success at this stage of your puppy's life is to set him up to win, and winning is having fun in a stress-free and safe environment such as I have described above.

Dog Parks

It would appear to be obvious that a dog park may be a suitable place for people who don't have access to a lot of personal space to take their dog for exercise. An example might be apartment dwellers or people who live in the major cities.

The second and possibly more widespread way of thinking (which I do not support) is that a dog park is a good place for a dog to socialize with other dogs.

Historically, dog parks have not been in existence all that long. It is believed that the first sanctioned dog park came into existence in the mid-1980s in Berkeley, California, and slowly began to catch on across the United States and beyond. I am sure the concept of a dog park was well intended, but in my opinion they are not such a great idea, especially when unruly dogs are allowed to run off-leash. The biggest problems that I see with off-leash dog parks are rooted in the fact that most people just do not understand dogs and have not established a pack structure or balance within their dogs. This means that most people's dogs are for the most part out of control. Over the years, I have heard about far too many tragic events occurring in dog parks. I personally would not take my dog to an off-leash dog park. In the blink of an eye, a peaceful afternoon can turn into a nightmare should another out-of-control and unbalanced dog begin to exhibit aggression.

Just like humans have bad days, even the most even-tempered dog can become aggravated enough to bite. The correct combination of stressful elements such as a strange or aggressive dog, not enough food or sleep, or even the desire to guard a favourite toy or person can result in dangerous behaviour. Dogs can also be injured during this off-leash park playtime, particularly if one dog is much larger or more rambunctious than the other.

Nearly all dog parks are designated as "use at your own risk." In theory, this means that everyone who uses the park has read the park rules, agrees to abide by them, and takes responsibility for their dog's actions. In doing so, the park owner is released from liability should an incident occur. According to these rules, every person who takes their dog(s) to an off-leash park is entirely responsible for their dogs' behaviour. Before entering a dog park, be sure to read the rules and restrictions associated with that park so that you are properly informed. In reality, many dog owners violate a park's rules by bringing in a dog that is not suited for such an environment. This can often consist of aggressive dogs, dogs that are not obedient, very young dogs, female dogs in heat, dogs that have not been vaccinated, or any combination of the preceding characteristics. Nearly all dog parks include a rule expressly forbidding aggressive dogs from using the facilities. The problem is that not all owners understand what constitutes an aggressive dog, or they downplay the behaviour. In cases where incidents occur as a result of broken park rules, it is best to notify the organization or municipality that oversees the park, and in rare cases where injury to you or your dog has occurred, you may even need to seek legal counsel.

People often question me on how to deal with overly aggressive dogs that belong to other pet owners who frequent local dog parks. They also inquire about their own dogs that might feel a need to defend themselves when approached by an apparently aggressive or unbalanced dog. Some people will ask if they should just let the dogs work these problems out themselves. There is no one correct response to such questions.

Today's typical dog owners do not take the time to learn and understand, much less implement the concept of pack structure. They don't understand just how deep-seated the pack instincts are that still exist in their family pets. These natural instincts can, and often do, become very apparent when a dog is taken into an environment occupied by other disobedient or unbalanced dogs (and owners). When a newcomer enters a park that other dogs visit every day, the new visitor is often regarded as an intruder into the "personal territory" of the regular visitor. More often than not, the new arrival is not perceived as a new found friend. This can often lead to either territorial aggression, dominance aggression, fear aggression, or any number of other undesirable behaviours.

Don't assume that every dog in the park is a well-mannered, well-trained pet. Just because it is playing with other dogs, it does not mean that it will play with your dog. The issue of rank has already been established with these other dogs, and the game may be going according to their rules. Your dog will not know the rules or necessarily readily accept the established ranking structure and can easily get into trouble.

Often I meet people who are disappointed in their puppy or young dog because it shies away from other dogs and chooses to avoid strange dogs it meets while on walks or in parks. Apparently, these people do not understand pack mentality; most may not even know that it exists. If you stop to think about it, normal people would never expect their young children to defend themselves against adults that were threatening their home. So why do people often expect their young dogs to confront older, more mature dogs?

The facts are that the majority of dogs have little or no desire to be pack leaders. They are completely content with their human owners assuming the role of a structured leader.

New puppy owners must realize that once a puppy—or even an adult dog—has been attacked by another dog, the likelihood of it becoming aggressive towards other dogs is heightened. This only has to happen one time for a permanent temperament change to occur in some animals. You will quickly find that dog-to-dog aggression is a real pain in the rear end. Far too many people with dominant dogs will still bring their dog to dog parks without first taking the necessary steps to get these dominance issues under control. If a person doesn't have the ability to control their dog's behaviour at home, or while out on a walk, what makes them think they will ever be able to control this same animal when it is off-leash at a dog park?

So are off-leash parks places you will want to frequent with your new puppy? I suggest they are not. However, I understand and respect the fact that this is a decision that will ultimately be made by each individual puppy's owner.

Doggy Daycare

Doggy daycares are quite common and are becoming more and more popular, especially these days when people tend to work longer hours and might even need to take on a second job to make ends meet. It is quite easy to feel guilty (or be made to feel guilty) about your dog not getting enough exercise or attention, so more and more frequently, people look to dog daycare to provide their dog(s) with what is often touted as being necessary social interaction and exercise. Can these trips to daycare cause more problems than they address? The short answer, I would have to say in my opinion, is "yes!"

Although I think dog daycares are great in theory, I maintain they are in reality a poor idea. I also believe that the owners of most dog daycares are caring, responsible people that truly love the dogs that they take care of. However, there are many reasons why dog daycares can be problematic, and that is what I want to address for you in this book. I am basing my hypothesis on over thirty-seven years of experience studying and training thousands of dogs. In countless interviews over the last decade or so (dog daycare is relatively new), many of my clients have identified behaviour changes occurring within timelines that are directly correlated to trips to the local doggy daycare. I have also witnessed, first-hand, dozens of incidents at an array of doggy daycares that I believe with certainty can lead to significant behavioural issues even if they only happen sporadically during visits. Based on my experiences, the problematic interactions that I witnessed occur more rather than less frequently.

I will always recommend dog walks instead of doggy daycare unless a dog has severe separation anxiety, as it is often called (I call it a behavioural issue), and cannot be left alone until the behaviour has been corrected. In that case, doggy daycare may be a temporary option until this behaviour can be addressed and the dog can be left alone for reasonable periods of time.

Here are some reasons that attending a dog daycare, in my opinion, can lead to behaviour problems.

Unbalanced dogs. Unfortunately, many dogs that visit doggy daycares are not well mannered or balanced. Dogs that are either unbalanced or have unusually dynamic play characteristics can create mayhem within a doggy daycare. Depending on the size, confidence level, or breed characteristics of your dog, he might develop undesirable play behaviours, become timid, or even become aggressive towards other dogs.

Little or no downtime. Some doggy daycares promote "cageless boarding" as a benefit. However, as you know, dogs, especially puppies, require an abundance of sleep. When dogs are subjected to a constant barrage of noise and the continuous movement of other energetic and barking dogs, they can often become exceedingly active for extended periods of time and that can lead to high stress levels within the dog. A dog that is under stress will often become less tolerant of other dogs or even humans, which may lead to an undesirable response to what would under normal circumstances be considered healthy interaction. Dogs subjected to such an environment—and without a means to retreat to a peaceful area—may even react aggressively towards other dogs. Many daycares do provide timeouts for their canine clients throughout the day; however, the dogs still cannot escape the sound of other barking dogs in the vicinity.

Employees' understanding of dog behaviour. Many doggy daycare attendants have insufficient experience in understanding dog body language and communication and therefore fail to recognize a problem developing before trouble actually occurs. I say this because I have been made aware of this happening over and over again, and I am often called upon to teach assistants how to deal with dogs and dog packs— but unfortunately usually not until after there has been an issue. When you consent to leave your dog in the care of daycare, you are assuming that the employees can, and will, identify problems before they start and skillfully prevent situations from escalating out of control, right? I have personal knowledge of daycares that will leave twenty to thirty, or even more, dogs of all sizes alone in a confined area to mingle without any supervision at all for extended periods of time. This is a ticking bomb just waiting for the right spark to detonate it. When problems do occur (and they will), often the dog's owner is told that their dog is not suited for doggy daycare. No kidding! Unless a dog is big enough and tough enough to rise to the top of the pack, most dogs are not suited to be dumped into this type of environment.

I have also witnessed more than one play session where one or more dogs are getting harassed, and no one intervenes. This situation can lead to dog's learning that they are on their own and will then respond by accelerating their behaviour by snapping, growling, or snarling at other dogs for self-preservation. These dogs will often start exhibiting this behaviour at home, or when any situation arises that makes them feel threatened.

I readily admit and accept that some people have used doggy daycare services for years with no problems. However, I am called on to assist with many dog-related problem behaviours that can be directly attributed to attending doggy daycare. The decision to take your dog to doggy daycare or not is yours and yours alone; however, I suggest you choose your doggy daycare carefully and watch your dog for any sudden development of undesirable behaviour traits that may be attributed to attending doggy daycare.

It is not my intention to tell you what to do with your puppy; my purpose herein is only to make you aware of potential issues and raise your awareness to what could and does happen. An informed decision is often a good decision.

Nipping

Let's begin this segment by being honest with ourselves: All puppies nip! They are not unlike little children. Everything seems to go into the mouth, including our fingers and toes. The problem, though, is that a puppy's teeth are like little needles and when they bite us, even in play, it hurts. Our job is not so much to teach the puppy that it can never put its mouth on us, but rather that if it insists on mouthing us, then it has to be done in a respectful and controlled fashion, and it must stop immediately when told to do so. And how might I do this, you are thinking? Well, if we can accept that dogs (even puppies) learn by association, then it becomes much easier to teach in a language that the puppy will understand. Think of it this way: If your puppy were to bite another puppy hard enough to hurt the other puppy, what would the other puppy do, especially if the other puppy was somewhat strong willed? Yes, it would let the offending puppy know when it was biting too hard, most likely by letting out a bit of a "yip" and probably by delivering a retaliatory bite in return. Now I don't expect you to bite your puppy. However, you must teach your puppy how and when to control his teeth if you hope for him to learn not to bite. The following is a description of what I recommend you do in order to teach your puppy not only how hard it is allowed to bite, but more importantly, to stop his or her chomping completely and immediately when told to do so.

I like to use the word "OUT" when I am teaching a puppy to stop a behaviour. The word "out," when spoken sharply and quickly, is very difficult to attach a negative connotation to. This word simply sounds like a short, sharp little bark, similar to what another dog might do. It certainly will get the puppy's attention. Keep in mind that this word is not to be used in a negative way but only to get your puppy's attention for just a moment so that he will look at you and stop whatever he is doing, which includes biting. Using the word "OUT" does not mean that whatever the puppy is doing was necessarily a bad thing; it merely lets him know that he is to stop whatever it is he is doing at the moment he hears the word. The instant he stops, then it is of utmost importance that you praise him for discontinuing the behaviour, regardless of what it was he was doing. Often the puppy will stop biting for only a few seconds and then go right back to gnawing at your fingers, toes, clothing, or whatever is in reach of those sharp little teeth. Now is the time you must assume a teaching role and let him know that you really did mean for him to stop biting. If you actually love your puppy, and I am sure that you do, then you really must love him enough to teach him right from wrong. In most cases, he no longer has the mother dog around to teach him proper behaviour. That task now falls squarely into your lap.

So let's assume that your puppy is biting at your fingers and is biting hard enough that it is becoming uncomfortable. Now is the time that you must begin to teach your puppy how hard he is allowed to bite and also that he must stop biting the instant you tell him to by using the word "OUT." Remember that in order to ensure that your puppy looks upon you as a firm but fair leader and teacher, you must refrain from repeating your commands. Unless he is deaf, he will hear you the first time. So when you tell him to stop biting by saying "OUT," and he does, you must immediately praise him both verbally and physically. This is the most important aspect of separating yourself from simply being a teacher into being a loved and well-respected great teacher, a teacher your puppy will learn to trust and respect no matter what. It may be necessary only to praise him sparingly so that he does not think this is a game and go right back to biting. You will have to be the judge as to how much praise is the right amount to reward him adequately but not so much so that it excites him to the extent he will go right back to biting. But wait, you told him to stop biting by using the word "OUT," and your puppy paid no attention whatsoever. Well if you were purposeful when you said "OUT" and your puppy ignores you, then it is time to assume the role of "lead dog." Keep in mind that a higher ranking sibling or an older dog would not accept your puppy disobeying their demand to stop biting or acting in an unacceptable fashion—neither should you. By now, I am sure you have accepted that dogs learn by association, so now is your chance to provide your puppy with an opportunity to associate disobeying your command with an adverse consequence. You were fair and kind every time he stopped his behaviour on previous occasions when you used the word "OUT." You must be equally fair and kind now, should he choose to disobey you. Being that your little bundle of fur and teeth is gnawing away at your fingers harder than what you are comfortable with, and he has chosen to continue to bite even after you had used the word "OUT," now is the time to take corrective action. Immediately and with appropriate intensity come up under the puppy's jaw with your index and middle finger and give him a sharp rap under the chin. If you do this smartly, you will find that your puppy will immediately stop biting. Now you must just as quickly praise him for ceasing his unacceptable behaviour. If you are dealing with a larger puppy, you may have to use a flattened hand/knuckle approach to deter the puppy from continuing to bite. Like everything we do, you must only tell him once, and then you need to take immediate and decisive action. If the first attempt is not successful, then you must increase the intensity of your corrections in a progressive manner. Don't be one who gets caught in the grip of temptation and thinks that giving him a second chance and telling him again will work. It will not. Now is the time to begin to partner with your puppy and earn his respect in a fair but firm and respectful manner. A puppy that will not listen to you when he is only a few months old surely will not listen to you when he begins to develop into an adult dog. In fact, that is the time when those who believe they can negotiate with their puppy, or coerce him into being a good canine citizen, will fully realize the folly of their absence of leadership and will often end up having to get rid of their dog (or worse) because they can no longer live with their very own dog. Dogs need leadership and structure and cannot function without them! Be fair to yourself and your dog. Provide the direction and structure your puppy craves! That's the least you can do for the dog you so desperately wanted in the first place. The aforementioned approach can be used to stop a dog from biting at your hands, feet, and clothing; it can even be used to get him to drop something he may have in his mouth.

Boundaries

Regardless of whether you live in a tiny apartment, a mansion, a sprawling ranch in the country, or somewhere in between, there will always be a need to establish some boundaries. Boundaries for your puppy may range from something as simple as showing him what areas of your home are out of bounds, to as complex as what part of your yard your puppy is not permitted to use as a bathroom area, teaching your puppy to stay out of a garden area, or helping him learn to stay within the perimeter of your property. Regardless of how few or how many boundaries you find it necessary to establish, it is ultimately your responsibility to take the time to ascertain appropriate boundary restrictions for your puppy. Although it is never too late to establish boundaries, the sooner you get started, the easier it usually is. If it is a very young puppy you are working with, you must keep in mind that you are training a baby, and therefore conduct yourself accordingly. You wouldn't expect a small child to understand a complex set of rules overnight, so you owe your puppy the same consideration— although puppies do learn much quicker than most humans. For the purpose of this book, we will use two examples of how to teach a puppy to stay within an established boundary. One example will pertain to an indoor boundary and the other a more challenging outdoor boundary.

Establishing an indoor boundary

For the purpose of this exercise, I will describe how to teach your puppy to stay out of a particular room in your home. To make it even easier we will make the assumption that the floor covering in the room you want your puppy to refrain from entering is different from the one he is allowed to walk upon. To start the teaching process, I would have a standard flat collar on my puppy and a light leash of any description, approximately 4 – 6 feet in length. Knowing that I am working with a young puppy I would be sure to take plenty of time in the teaching process; if you are one with limited patience, perhaps you should pick a day when you are in a particularly good mood to start this process.

I would recommend beginning by gently taking the puppy to the visible

Regular Flat Collar

dividing line between the two rooms, which in this case will be evident by the differences in the floor covering (carpet to hardwood, for example). I would point to the dividing line between the two rooms and gently but firmly talk to the puppy while I patiently walk him along the entire length of the border between the two rooms. While you are doing this, you can tell your puppy anything you like; just make sure, though, that you speak in a calm but firm tone of voice. It is very important that while you are introducing your puppy to this boundary he is never allowed to touch the floor covering in the room you no longer want him to enter. Once you have introduced your puppy to the border between the two rooms and have spoken to him calmly and firmly while guiding him along the entire length of the border, gently turn and lead him away. The very instant that you turn your puppy away from that dividing line, you must immediately and emphatically praise him. I ask that you be kind and patient while introducing your puppy to this exercise as he may not yet have any idea what it is that you are trying to convey to him. This is why you must exercise patience when teaching a puppy this exercise. What you need to establish in the puppy's mind is that there is something about that dividing line that causes you to become very stern, but as soon as you/ he turn(s) away from it, all becomes great again. You are laying the all important groundwork that will allow the puppy to "connect the dots" a bit later on. Perform this exercise at least one time per day for at least four days in a row. If you do it twice a day for four consecutive days, that will be okay as well; however, do not do it more than twice a day. More is not better. It is also important that during these four days of etching this boundary into your puppy's mind, he is never allowed to go into this room. If for some reason you let your guard down and you find him in the room, you must remove him immediately and very sternly take him from the room and then praise him immediately once he crosses the border from one room to the other. Following four days of this persistent and patient teaching, you will then be ready to advance to the next step, and that is allowing your puppy to learn in the very way nature intended him to learn, and that is by association.

Before you begin this next phase of boundary training, I ask that you make sure your puppy is wearing his flat collar. Now take a short piece of cord or light rope (a sports shoelace works well) and attach it to his collar and allow it to drag along the floor behind him. This simple but effective apparatus will allow you to catch the puppy quickly should he decide to turn this all important exercise into a game.

On the fifth day of your boundary training exercise, you will now begin to hold the puppy responsible for his actions. This is to say that after four days of patiently showing your puppy the boundary and giving him ample opportunity to associate your stern warnings with the boundary anytime that he is in close proximity to it, your puppy will now be allowed to make the following choices: Do I avoid the boundary or do I not? If he chooses to avoid the boundary and not cross over it, that is exactly the behaviour you are looking for, so you must praise him for staying on the desired side of the boundary. If, however, he chooses to ignore your four days of coaching and teaching and proceeds to pass right over the boundary as if it had no meaning, then you must now provide a slightly negative consequence for him doing so. This is the point where the cord that you previously attached to his collar will come in handy. The very instant his first little paw contacts the floor on the side of the boundary that you do not want him to be on, you must spring into action. Be decisive and quick as you move toward him and immediately take hold of the dragging rope and with conviction reverse his direction right back over the boundary to the proper side. He may act startled at first, however, don't concern yourself with that. He has had several days to learn and familiarize himself with the boundary.

Introducing the puppy to a boundary.

Before commencing this next and final stage of your puppy's boundary training exercise, I cannot stress enough that if you still possess that inert human compulsion to insert that useless word "NO" into your training, you must stop it now. Using the word "no" serves little or no useful purpose in your dog's education. It is a word that is repeatedly used to no avail. The one and only thing that you will ever accomplish with using that negative expression is to teach your dog two things: (a) that you are truly not a good leader and are negative inside; and (b) that you truly don't mean what you say, especially if you repeat yourself. Remember what it is that you are attempting to teach your puppy—that stepping across that boundary line will result in an undesirable consequence, and it is never you that is negative. Saying "NO" to your puppy is negative, and it is coming from you. Therefore, it does not take an animal long to realize that the source of the word is negative, not the word itself. You must remain positive at all times. Your puppy will love you for it.

Now you are going show your puppy what you were trying to convey to him when you spoke in your stern voice each time he went near the border during the first four days when you were introducing him to the boundary. The instant he is back on the correct side of the boundary, you must enthusiastically praise your puppy so that he now experiences the positive consequence of returning to the right side of the boundary. Your puppy can now experience and relate to a negative experience on one side of the border and a positive experience on the other. Puppies, because they learn by association, will learn this very quickly. Your puppy will immediately associate the negative consequence with crossing over the borderline. Just as quickly, he will associate the positive experience of staying on the correct side of the boundary with the place where he gets all your love and affection. Puppies learn very quickly, so don't be fooled into thinking he's forgotten that he shouldn't step into the room that you took so much time to patiently teach him to stay out of. He does not forget! Oh, he may disobey and enter the forbidden room just to see if maybe you have forgotten or if you will take pity on him, but I can assure you he did not forget that he is not supposed to be there. If you are persistent and fair in your teachings, in a matter of just a few days you will begin to enjoy the benefits of a puppy who understands and accepts where he can and cannot wander around within the confines of your home. By teaching and introducing structure by way of adopting a fair but firm approach, you are also skillfully establishing a mutual and respectful bond between you and your puppy that will be invaluable in the years to come.

Establishing an outdoor boundary

You will be able to establish an outdoor boundary in precisely the same manner as you did for indoor boundaries. Understand that outdoor areas are usually considerably more exciting and often much larger, so teaching a puppy or young dog outdoor boundaries can be slightly more challenging and may take a bit more time and patience. For instance, if you want your puppy to be able to use one part of your yard but not enter into another area, it might understandably be somewhat more difficult for the puppy to grasp the difference when both areas are covered in the same layer of soft green grass. In this case, I would put up a temporarily visible boundary—such as some little flags or even a garden hose stretched between the two areas—for the puppy to utilize as a visible guide. This visible reference does not have to be permanent. With proper coaching, any dog can be taught to take advantage of some areas and to avoid others. I would also recommend teaching the outdoor boundaries after you have mastered teaching the indoor boundaries. There are two reasons for this. First, both you and your puppy now have some experience in working with boundaries, and second, your puppy will now be a bit older and therefore will absorb information at a faster pace. Regardless of what boundaries you are attempting to establish, always follow the four fundamental rules of dog training: (1) tell him—don't ask him; (2) don't tell him more than once; (3) always be in a position to enforce your commands (have a leash on your dog); and (4) keep your training fun.

Puppy Training Classes

Time and time again I receive calls from well-meaning people asking me if I offer puppy training classes. I don't offer such classes for a couple of reasons. First, if we are talking about puppies only a few months old (8 – 16 weeks or so), we all recognize that the duration of their attention span is measured in mere minutes, if not seconds. Do you really want to pay someone to teach your puppy for a few moments at a time over the course of several weeks, when you can do the same thing in the comfort of your own home by following the instructions in this book? Second, there is not a whole lot in the way of reliable obedience that you will be able to teach a young puppy (less than five to six months of age) that he will not challenge you on when he reaches six to eight months of age and beyond. My belief is that rather than pushing a puppy harder than what is reasonable at such a tender age, it is far more advantageous to focus on what we can accomplish; namely, learning the dos and don'ts of nurturing a puppy. Puppy classes are often marketed as valuable socialization classes as well. I have never been convinced that there is a whole lot of long-term value in allowing your puppy to romp and play with other puppies that are just as foolish as yours may be. I believe there is a better way, and that is why I have written this book, which is intended to provide you with the information you need to shape your puppy's behaviour during the first few months of his life.

Grooming

As there is such a wide range of dog breeds (many of which require specialized grooming services that only a professional groomer can provide), I am going to limit this information to the everyday grooming necessities required for any dog, regardless of the breed. One of the most basic grooming needs that so many dog owners struggle with is trimming their dog's toe nails. Although I do not profess that it is an absolute necessity that you do your own dog's nail trimming, I do believe that there are many benefits of doing so—aside from the obvious cost savings.

To begin with, as you may or may not have already experienced, most dogs do not initially take kindly to having their nails cut. To minimize the resistance your dog may exhibit, it is always a good idea to get in the habit of touching and gently squeezing your dog's paws right from the first day you bring him home. Although handling a dog's paws does not always translate into the puppy liking his nails being cut, it certainly will not do any harm. Cutting your puppy's nails can be compared to going to the dentist. It is not something that most of us look forward to or enjoy; however, it is something we have to tolerate for our own good health. Likewise, your puppy does not have to enjoy getting his nails cut; however, it is something that he must learn to tolerate. Whether it is you, his own trusted friend, cutting his nails or a stranger in a grooming shop, having his nails trimmed is a necessary nuisance for most dogs. The reason I encourage dog owners to cut their own puppy's nails is that it is a useful way to teach dogs at a very young age that from time to time they may be subjected to things they do not like or agree with; however, they must learn to respect you enough to trust in your judgement as the great leader you are, and put up with having their nails cut. If you see this first nail cutting exercise through to the end and stay calm and be patient with your puppy, this initial and often somewhat unpleasant experience will go a long way to further reinforcing your abilities as a leader and will elevate your puppy's trust in you to a whole new level.

Whatever you do during this first nail cutting attempt, do not scold or in any way become upset with your puppy. This is one of the single best exercises to demonstrate to your puppy that regardless of how much he protests, you will not be swayed. As upsetting as this may be to your puppy, he will bounce right back to normal the moment you have cut the last nail. The only difference will be that he now truly knows that you are a leader he can trust and respect. Take advantage of this opportunity to build upon your relationship with your puppy. I might add that you just might come out of this with a whole new appreciation for your puppy's resolve, as well as a vastly improved level of self-control and self-patience.

Most dogs will, from time to time, require that you check and clean their ears. Most dogs do not like this much at all; however, I am sure if it were up to dogs, they would choose this over having their nails cut. Try to get in the habit of having a peek inside your dog's ears on a regular basis to see if they are inflamed or are particularly dirty. If your puppy is scratching his ears excessively, you detect any foul odor coming from your puppy's ears, or his ears look red or inflamed, start by taking a soft cloth with a mixture of white vinegar and water mixed at a ratio of 10:1 (one part vinegar and ten parts water) and gently swab the interior of your dog's ears. Be gentle but persistent when cleaning your dog's ears because although he doesn't have to like getting his ears cleaned, he does have to learn to tolerate it without putting up a fuss or becoming aggressive. If at any time you feel that your puppy might have an ear infection or any other inner ear issue or is incessantly scratching at his ears, always consult your veterinarian. Veterinarians are the experts and are trained to diagnose ear issues that most of us simply do not have the expertise to diagnose or address.

All dogs, young and old alike, should be exposed to having their coat brushed on a regular basis. Start brushing your puppy just as soon as practicable once he has settled into his new home with your family. Choose a brush or grooming mitt that is suitable for your dog's coat, but whatever you do don't brush too aggressively. If you encounter knots in your dog's coat, slowly work them out by applying a detangler treatment and then slowly and carefully brush the knots out. If for some reason the tangled hair is matted to the point where it forms a clump, it may be advisable to carefully cut out the mat. In any case, be careful not to cause your dog any pain so that he does not develop an adversity to having his coat brushed. If done properly and in a gentle manner, most dogs actually learn to like having their coat brushed as it feels good to them. Once again, remain calm, and whatever you do you must be patient.

Visitors

Although we all want our puppy to be excited and happy to meet new people or visitors in our home, we must also take steps to ensure that our puppy learns how to respectfully greet people. Jumping up, nipping, and/or bouncing all over them are not acceptable greeting behaviours, even though most puppies will do just that. The time to teach your puppy appropriate conduct, which includes acceptable behaviour when meeting people, is now. A puppy that gets overly excited and barks, jumps up, or does a multitude of other things is not always viewed as being "cute." Perhaps while they are still very young this kind of behaviour may appear cute or be acceptable to some people; however, as your puppy grows and becomes more determined, this type of behaviour will quickly become a nuisance. Don't be fooled into thinking that your puppy will outgrow this behaviour, as so many might lead you to believe. Unless you teach your puppy proper manners, this undesirable behaviour will only worsen as he gets older.

Jumping up on people is one of the most common but undesirable behaviours exhibited by puppies. Once we learn to recognize why puppies develop this impolite tendency in the first place, it is always much easier to eliminate the behaviour. Puppies, for the most part, are very friendly and social creatures, and as such they are very difficult to ignore when they seek attention by jumping on people. That in itself is also the key to teaching a puppy not to jump up on people in order to get attention. Those of us who are inclined to tell the puppy to get down, push the puppy down, or even bump the puppy with their knee, are often inadvertently giving the puppy precisely what he wants, attention. When a puppy jumps up and we acknowledge the puppy in any way, we are actually encouraging the puppy to jump. What we as humans may construe as a negative consequence, a puppy will often perceive as positive attention. If we say anything at all to the puppy, make eye contact with it, or touch it by pushing it down, we are actually reinforcing and thus encouraging the very behaviour we want to curb. If you can accept that all dogs, even puppies, learn by association rather than by repetition, then it is actually quite easy to teach a puppy, or any other dog for that matter, not to jump up. What you must do, though, is transform the act of jumping up so that it is no longer viewed as a positive behaviour from your puppy's point of view, but rather an action that brings about a negative consequence. To do so effectively, we must remain calm, assertive, and confident at all times.

Bear in mind that puppies live in a world of legs. This is to say that as a puppy they are often surrounded by people's legs which are continually moving, starting and stopping without any advance warning. It is also important to comprehend why puppies greet us by jumping on us in the first place, and that is to gain our attention. When teaching a puppy not to jump on us, these two factors can work to our advantage. Your mission is to convince the puppy that you cannot see him unless you have acknowledged him and that you might start to walk without any advance notice. Therefore, the moment your puppy jumps up on you, or better still, is in the act of jumping up on you, you must step forward abruptly and bump right into him. I cannot stress enough that you must not look down or communicate with your puppy in any way. You need to time your step forward so that it coincides with your puppy jumping up and carefully bump into him with the top of your foot. Consider that in your puppy's mind, your legs moving are a perfectly natural occurrence. What comes as a surprise to him and what he cannot understand is why you did not see him. It goes without saying that your puppy's bid for attention did not work out quite the way he had hoped, even though it may have succeeded in the past. Now puppies being puppies, and being incredibly intelligent, will almost immediately try to find another way to gain your attention. Invariably, all puppies will move back and forth in front of you, all the while doing their very best to get your attention. Do not acknowledge him in any way, not yet. It should only take but a few seconds before your puppy in his quest to get your attention will sit in front of you. Presto, now your eyesight returns, and you will instantly acknowledge him by dropping down to his level and petting and praising him. If he jumps again repeat the process until your puppy will quickly sit and wait for you to acknowledge him. Your puppy has just learned how to get the very thing he craves, your attention. It will become immediately apparent that when he wants your attention, he will approach and sit down in front of you. Do not pass up this opportunity to reward this behaviour. In your puppy's mind, jumping up did not bring about the desired reaction from you. However, he has learned that he can solicit a positive response from you and others by approaching and sitting quietly in front of you. If you have three or four friends who are willing to help you with this exercise, you will curb your puppy's desire to jump on people almost immediately.

Educating your puppy will often include educating visitors to your home so that they can also contribute to your puppy's learning, if in no other way than to refrain from inadvertently rewarding your puppy for jumping up in the first place. Teach your family, friends, and visitors not to acknowledge the puppy in a positive way if he jumps up on them. Visitors should also be taught how to interact with a puppy. Visitors who immediately, upon entering your home, excitedly engage your puppy and make a big fuss over him are actually making it much more difficult for you to teach your puppy proper manners. If you have visitors who will not or do not follow your instructions on how to interact with your puppy, then you may have to be more insistent or in some cases even put the puppy away prior to their arrival or immediately following their arrival. This, however, is not the desired action because putting your puppy away when people come to your home can in some cases actually bring out aggressive behaviours towards visitors to your home as the puppy grows and develops. It is always to your advantage to focus on educating your puppy and the people he regularly interacts with rather than keeping them separate.

Summary

In conclusion, I wish to reiterate the importance of beginning to teach a puppy good manners or good canine behaviour at an early age. This way, you can shape the puppy's behaviour so that not only will he be a well-behaved and considerate member of your family, but he will also become a respected and good canine citizen within your community. Keep in mind that puppies will do only what comes naturally to them as they develop their communication and survival skills. In today's rapidly changing world, the world in which your puppy must learn to live and thrive, many natural canine behaviours are simply not acceptable. Although dogs as direct descendants of wolves started becoming domesticated some 10,000 or more years ago, many of their primal instincts are still very powerful. In order for a dog to flourish in our human world, it is our responsibility to teach them acceptable manners and behaviour skills. Most puppies will exhibit behaviours that directly reflect the environment in which they live and the actions of those with whom they are in direct contact with. I always recommend that we educate a puppy or dog of any age rather than regulate or attempt to control the dog's behaviour. Remember that all dogs first learn by association and then develop skills or behaviours by repeating them. Therefore, if a dog repeats a behaviour that we find undesirable, we must find a way to get the puppy to associate such behaviour with an adverse consequence. Conversely, we must attach a positive result with desirable behaviours or actions so that the dog associates this desirable behaviour with a positive outcome and is therefore more likely to repeat that behaviour.

The trainer's primary responsibility is simply to allow a dog to experience the consequences of each behaviour the dog exhibits. Dogs must be allowed to make choices. That is how they learn in the most efficient way. The trainer's responsibility is to monitor and guide a dog's choices in such a way as to protect the dog from harm should it make poor decisions but also allow the dog to experience the consequences of their behaviours. In the case of unacceptable or undesirable choices, we as teachers must allow the dog to experience a negative outcome but only to the extent that the dog experiences some discomfort or unexpected results without experiencing any injury to himself. Nature is a harsh but effective teacher. We will never take the place of nature's effective way of teaching to ensure the survival of only the most intelligent and/or strongest. However, we should always do our best to utilize the successful ways of nature in order to teach in a controlled and effective manner. Never deprive your dog of an opportunity to learn. Encourage your dog to learn under your watchful eye, and allow your puppy to experience and learn from all that life has to offer.

References

Volhard, Jack, and Wendy Volhard. 2010. *Dog Training for Dummies, 3rd Edition*. New Jersey: Wiley Publishing, Inc.

Volhard, Wendy, and Kerry Brown, D.V.M. 2000. *Holistic Guide for a Healthy Dog, Second Edition*. California: Howell Book House.

Index

*Note: Page numbers in **bold** indicate photographs.*

www.ingramcontent.com/pod-product-compliance
Lightning Source LLC
Chambersburg PA
CBHW071455070426
42452CB00039B/1362